Lucy Herd

9 Stanley Avenue

Hornsea
E Yks

to Dr Alfred Dwrley.
with Greetings
for Xmas

GOD AND MY NEIGHBOUR

God and My Neighbour

by

H. R. L. SHEPPARD, C.H., D.D.

*Canon and Precentor of St. Paul's
Cathedral, Chaplain to H.M. the King,
lately Vicar of St. Martin-in-the-
Fields, and Dean of Canterbury.*

CASSELL & CO., LTD.

London   Melbourne

Toronto   Sydney

First edition   .   November 1937
Second edition .   December 1937
Third edition   .   December 1937

PRINTED IN GREAT BRITAIN BY
EBENEZER BAYLIS AND SON, LTD., THE
TRINITY PRESS, WORCESTER, AND LONDON
1237

PREFACE

TO any one who stops to think, the world to-day must seem a pretty grim place. The voice of brotherhood is drowned by the din of the armourer's forge—and the new and more terrible weapons with which science has armed man for his own destruction are already being used against civilian populations in wars of an unexampled ferocity. The horrors of Canton and Nanking, and the martyrdom of Spain, are a stern reminder of how slight is our hold upon civilization.

While the shadow of strife thus lies heavy upon the nations, there are men and women—and little children—who never have enough food, or sufficient warm clothing. Unemployment has been reduced—but there are still too many willing hands that can find no work to do.

There are those who prefer to shut their eyes to such things. There are others, alas, who cannot. Want and despair are their life—the only life they have known for years.

Against this sombre background, the articles reproduced in these pages may seem trivial and irrelevant. I can imagine a reader exclaiming: "Is this all that Christianity has to offer us in these days when the world stands at the cross-roads?"

The answer is, of course, that these articles are

not, in any sense, a statement of the Christian faith. Christianity is very much more than appears here. It is very much more than, even with far greater gifts of eloquence and scholarship than I possess, I could begin to say, were I to attempt to put my creed upon paper.

There is only one way in which we can really learn what Christianity is, what it requires of us, and what it offers to the world and to the individual soul. We must go to the Gospels, to the words of Our Lord Himself. And we must not only read, we must ponder them. We must steep ourselves in those profound simplicities that are as fresh and vital to-day, amid the roar and bustle of our great cities, as they were, two thousand years ago, upon the hills of Galilee.

We shall find, in the teaching of Christ, many hard sayings. The way of life to which He calls us is not easy. There is in it no place for compromise. But what a mess we have made of the world, trying to evade the practical consequences of the creed we profess—and how different it would be if our Christianity was real, and not a sham!

These articles, written, week by week, for The *Sunday Express*, only touch, here and there, upon these great issues. In the main, they deal with simple, everyday problems of conduct and character. But they try to bring those problems to the touchstone of the Christian spirit. And I hope that they may, perhaps, encourage readers to rediscover for themselves the fountainhead of Christianity in the pages of the Gospels.

If they do that even in one or two cases, they will have justified themselves.

H. R. L. Sheppard.

1 Amen Court,
   St. Paul's,
     E.C.

CONTENTS

"HOW fed up and disillusioned you must be," a man said to me the other day.

He was an intellectual—a believer in reason and logic, and the power of mind over multitude.

"Progress!" was his watch-word, and, like many another, he had thought of the onward and upward march of man as something inevitable.

It might be delayed or held up occasionally—but it could not be stemmed.

Now he was no longer sure. Over a large part of the world the things to which he held—democracy, freedom of speech and thought, the rule of reason, liberty, humane culture—had been destroyed. Not only had the forward movement been interrupted, but civilization was in full retreat.

It was with all this in mind that he said to me: "How fed up and disillusioned you must be."

"Not nearly so disillusioned as you are," I replied. "You have nothing else. I have."

I said that because, although in many ways we thought alike and sought similar ends, there was one essential difference between us.

In his philosophy there was no room for God. He saw in man only the product of a blind evolution—and beyond this present life he could discern nothing but eternal darkness.

In his sky there was no Star of Bethlehem.

But for me, as for all who accept the Christian message, this life is not the whole.

The grave has no power over the soul. Death is not an end, but a beginning.

So, while we desire to make the world a better place, and hate to see it blundering blindfold to the pit, we do not despair.

There is one hope of which no tyranny can rob us, which no disaster can destroy—the hope of the Hereafter.

And though men may let us down, we know that God will not fail us. Our faith and our trust are in Him.

From Him, even in the darkest hour, we draw strength and courage.

We have faith also in His purpose. We do not understand that purpose,

> . . . yet we trust that somehow good
> Will be the final goal of ill,

and believe, even in the midst of apparent chaos, in

> . . . one far-off divine event
> To which the whole creation moves.

The typical intellectual is a sceptic. For him there is no purpose in the universe.

But he did believe, for a time, in human

intelligence—and that human intelligence was going to solve the world's problems.

By keeping his mind fixed on that, and working to help along the progress he conceived to be irresistible, he was able to find life worth while.

To-day, that is all changed.

I meet a good many of these intellectuals. For the most part, their mood at present is one of utter hopelessness and pessimism.

There are a number of them who imagined that a new social order was being fashioned in Russia.

They did not altogether like some of the aspects of the Soviet experiment, but they were prepared to excuse a great deal on the grounds of "revolutionary necessity."

The main thing, they said, was that here was Socialism in practice. As its benefits became apparent, Socialism would sweep the world.

Recent events in Russia have disillusioned them.

The Communist land of promise has been revealed as an Oriental despotism, where criticism is crime and the whisper of an informer means sentence of death.

There are other intellectuals who pinned their faith to some change in economic organization.

They preached, with burning enthusiasm, their own universal cure-all—monetary reform, national planning, "New Deals," and so on.

No doubt they still believe in these things, but they are no longer confident of their ability to convert others to their point of view. And they are beginning to doubt whether any of these, in itself, would be sufficient—whether the world can be saved by economic means alone.

But they have nothing else to offer—either to us or to themselves.

Yet another group saw in the advance of physical science the salvation of mankind.

Their thoughts are otherwise to-day as they listen to the drone of the warplanes overhead or read of experiments with poison gas.

One by one the dreams of the intellectuals have been exploded. And they have nothing left.

They peer into the remote future—and see only the grim vision of the world and the universe running down like a watch.

The onward march of humanity has become a procession to final extinction.

To the Christian it doesn't matter whether the physical universe is doomed or not.

He looks beyond the physical appearance to the spiritual reality. He knows that the soul is immortal and that all things are in the hands of God.

That means a great deal here and now.

It means that the Christian is able to go on working for what he believes to be right without bothering too much about what the result of his efforts is going to be.

He follows the truth that is in him—and leaves the rest to God.

It is significant that to-day the only people in

Germany who can call their souls their own are the Christians, of whatever denomination, who have refused to accept the dictation of the State on matters of religion.

We hear nothing to-day of the German intellectuals. But we hear a great deal of the men and women to whom, even under Nazi rule, God means more than Hitler.

Science has placed new and more terrible weapons at the disposal of men. But his greatest force in the world is still conscience.

Conscience is on the march in Germany. Twenty years of persecution have failed to kill Christianity in Russia.

Looking at these things, and thinking of the great host of humble folk who, in all the countries of the world, live, to the best of their ability, Christian lives, I cannot give way to despair.

The intellectual, indeed, may be disillusioned. He may abandon the unequal contest.

But the Christian knows that God is with him, even in the Valley of the Shadow of Death.

He knows also that, to save mankind, no theory or "ism" will be of any avail, but only a change of heart.

It is the realization of that which has made the intellectual despair. But it cannot daunt the Christian. For God can change the hearts of men.

RECENTLY, when writing about the "recall to religion," I asked the question: "What religion?"

The average person in this country would answer without hesitation: "The religion of Jesus Christ." But ask for details and you will probably get widely divergent replies.

What is, in fact, the religion of our Lord Jesus Christ? What was the great contribution that He made to religion?

It wasn't just going about being nice to people, or healing the sick, or holding out the hand of friendship to prostitutes so that they might start afresh, or feeding five thousand with a few scraps.

These things all had a lovely significance. They have still a meaning and encouragement for us to-day. But the heart of our Lord's Message is not in them.

It lies in the exciting statement—to give which to the world He lived and died—that God, Who was a mystery, as in essence He still is a mystery to us, is our Father, and that therefore all men, everywhere, whatever their nation, or race, or colour, are brothers one of another.

6

We know the love of a father for his children. We know what it means to be brothers of the same blood and bone. We know the strength and sweetness of family ties.

So this message comes home to us. Or it would come home if we didn't take it so much for granted that we never stop to think of what it really means.

But it was a new idea to the men and women of His time. And those of us who rediscover it to-day experience the same shock of surprise at its sweeping implications, respond instinctively to its lovely warm humanity, feel its transfiguring power.

There has never been any teaching so effective in changing men's lives and making them vital and significant. There has never been any teacher at once so human and so compelling.

But we must listen to what He has to say to us. We must, of ourselves and in our own hearts, make this rediscovery of the Fatherhood of God, and all that follows from it, as something that affects us personally, because of which we can never be the same again.

I should say that if, in Britain, we really want a recall to religion, it is for this that we should pray. If, by recall to religion, we mean a return to the values and standards of Jesus Christ, the first and last thing we have got to realize is that we mustn't merely give lip service to the Brotherhood of Man.

If we once can feel this sense of brotherhood, instead of merely talking about it, many things will take on a new aspect and a new colour. All war, for instance, will seem to us civil war—a war of brothers. A battlefield will be as dreadful as a home turned into a shambles by the sudden madness of those who live in it.

But there is much more to it than that. We pray for the preservation of peace—but peace isn't just an absence of bomb-throwing.

There can be no peace in Britain, even if there is never another war, while the men and women of the depressed areas still lie under the blight of unemployment, feel the pinch of semi-starvation.

There can be no peace in Britain while wealth flaunts its luxury in the face of want, while class hatred and class bitterness poison the springs of human relationships.

There can be no peace in Britain while there is cruelty, and malice, and greedy self-seeking; while strength grabs the things it covets and weakness goes to the wall.

There can be no peace without sacrifice.

There can be no peace without mutual understanding, and mutual trust, and mutual helpfulness.

Above all, there can be no peace without love.

If we are really in earnest about the recall to religion, we must stand for the values which Jesus Christ stood for. We can't do that by being sentimental or even by prayer.

We can only do it by living, so far as we can, in the light of our Lord's teaching and in the spirit of His message to mankind.

It is not necessary, if we do that, to talk or preach about it overmuch. Our lives will speak for themselves, because they will be hall-marked with reality, with sacrifice for the brethren.

Where, then, do the Churches come in?

Obviously, we are all very human. We have our times of weakness, of doubt, of despair.

We put our hand to the plough, and then we get tired in the middle of driving our furrow. We need to be kept up to scratch.

We need to be reminded of our ideals—and of our duties and responsibilities as Christians. We need spiritual repair.

Nobody can criticize the presentation of Christianity by the Churches more easily than I can. I know their failures and their blind spots a great deal better then the uninformed layman who sometimes says bitter things about them.

Often enough, indeed, these people are criticizing something that isn't now as it was when they knew it many years ago.

But, for most of us, some form of Christian fellowship, some public profession of faith, some rite of worship in which we can join with our neighbours, is a necessity.

I confess that, unless the Churches are sincerely standing for values that are really Christian— for the love of God and the Brotherhood of Man,

which issues in the life of service—they are of no
use in this modern world.

Nothing but real Christianity—vital, tremendous, all-compelling—can help us. In a situation
such as that in which we are to-day religion has
to be tremendous or nothing.

At the moment we who call ourselves Christians
aren't sufficiently alive.

Communists, Fascists, the people who beat the
big drums of national patriotism or imperialist
ambition, have collared all the enthusiasm. For
multitudes of people some political creed has
taken the place of religion; some dictator or party
leader is the only god they know.

If it is to become a reality, the recall to religion
to which we pay lip service must strike the
prophetic note. It must not be utilitarian. It
must not be linked up with narrow national
sentiment. It must not be complacent. We must
cross from our side to God's.

We must realize, too, that we aren't going to
popularize Christianity. The demands that
Christ makes on those who would serve Him are
too big. And a pale, anæmic revival of conven-
tional religion, which hasn't, for many a year,
made conditions satisfactory for the majority of
those who should be the Churches' charge and
care, is of no use to-day.

But a real recall to religion will test the sincerity
of those who now so lightly give it their vote.

Do the leaders of Christendom really mean

business—or do we? I await eagerly, expectantly, the voice of prophecy.

It will be extremely offensive to Colonel Blimp. But it may save the world. There is nothing else that can.

AN American visitor was being shown round
our House of Commons. He asked his guide
what the chaplain did. "Does he pray for the
members?"

"No," was the reply. "He comes in, looks
round at the members, and then prays for the
country."

It may be an old story, but I like it. Some of the
best fellows I know are in Parliament, but that's
how I feel about a good many of the others. And
judging from conversations I've had recently with
all sorts and conditions of people, and by the
comments in my daily letter-bag, I'm not alone
in this attitude.

The enthusiasm has gone out of politics. In
its place there are disillusion and disgust.

I cannot recollect a time when the prestige of
the politicians has fallen so low.

Partly, no doubt, the trouble is due to the
Government's uneasy juggling with hot plates
over the Abyssinian question. But it goes deeper
than that: the thing that has really damned
politics in the eyes of the public is their insincerity.

With some honourable exceptions there seems
to be no M.P. who believes passionately in any-

thing. The majority are jockeying for position—playing the good old political game.

The Duke of Wellington said that the battle of Waterloo was won on the playing-fields of Eton.

The twentieth century has a sterner and more difficult battle to fight—a battle against poverty, against insecurity of employment and the evils it breeds, against all the blind fears and hatreds and jealousies that ferment and fester in the hearts of men and poison the relations of classes and nations.

And that battle will never be won playing the party game in Parliament.

I don't want to be misunderstood. I believe in constitutional government.

I believe that parties have a useful function to fulfil in the working of democratic institutions.

But the parties must stand for something real and vital in our national life. They must have the courage for creative action. They must face problems and tackle them, not just look at them sideways and put them carefully back on the shelf again.

It is because no party seems to be doing this, because they are all tarred with the same brush of time-serving and timidity, that popular opinion is so fed up with politics and politicians.

Yet, talk to them separately, get them away from politics, and all the politicians are decent enough. Their standard of personal honour is high. They're not grafters. Many of them, indeed, lose money by staying in public life.

Well, then, what's wrong?
There seems to be a poison in politics. It gets different people in different ways—but it gets most of them.

It takes one man of real charm and culture and turns him into an animated bogy, bent on frightening the nation out of its wits.

It has paralysed another—once trusted by the whole nation—and left him incapable of anything but playing a curious sort of political patience in which the cards never come out right, and which he is always having to start all over again.

But I'm afraid that the effects of this poison are often worst in the case of the private member.

He goes up to Westminster for the first time, perhaps still young, with convictions, principles, a sense of responsibility to the people who have sent him, a determination to do what he can for them.

He quickly decides that, beyond helping an individual now and again, there is really nothing he can do for them.

He finds that principles and convictions count for very little against the claims of party loyalty.

He rarely gets a chance to speak. When he does, there is practically no one to listen to him.

Very soon he learns that the smoking-room is a pleasanter place than the debating chamber. Unless there are fireworks to be enjoyed—when

L. G., or Winston, or Jimmie Maxton is "up"—there is no reason why he should be in the House.

The division bell will ring when he is wanted and the Whips will tell him how to vote.

If it were any use kicking he'd kick, he tells you. But it's no good. He's absolutely helpless. So he takes the line of least resistance.

And presently he doesn't mind his impotence so much. A year or two more, and perhaps he doesn't mind at all.

It is a simple thing to succumb to the occupational diseases of politics—fatty degeneration of the will, hardening of the heart, cirrhosis of the conscience. God help those who do, and God help the country over which they rule.

Even here in this fair country millions are existing on the border-line of destitution, millions don't get enough to eat. The death-rate among the unemployed and the most poorly paid workers is roughly double what it is among the rest of us. The Means Test is increasing the area of semi-starvation and breaking up the family circle. Farmers are fined for selling milk too cheaply to those who need it most. Even slum clearance may merely increase disease, if better homes mean higher rents and less money to spend on food.

And yet Parliament seems to do nothing. Can you wonder that—even apart from foreign affairs—the people of Britain are weary of politics?

There is no leadership, no grappling greatly with great problems.

Yet the problems are not insoluble. They can't be in a world where there is a super abundance of every kind of food and when, in our own land, there are empty acres and idle money—and idle men.

There is plenty of good will in all classes. Given a Government with guts, what a change could be worked in England!

Oh, for a few more men in Parliament with the courage to crusade against coffin houses—the houses with the empty larders and the wolf inside the door—as Samuel Plimsoll crusaded against coffin ships!

SOME of us are meeting the Jarrow marchers. We are to talk to them. What are we to say?

Are we to tell these men who have walked 260 miles from a town where one man in every two is unemployed, who are footsore and weary, many of whom have been without work or hope for many years, who have lived with despair and supped on bitterness, that they have no business in London—that they ought to have stayed at home?

Are we to tell them, with the Bishop of Durham, that in marching to the capital to present a petition to Parliament they are being "revolutionary"—that they are "substituting for the provisions of the Constitution the method of organized mob pressure?"

Or are we, like certain other Churchmen, to bless and ban in the same breath these patient men who have endured and suffered so much— to say we know they mean no harm, but that, of course, we can't really approve?

Well, I'll admit that this march of the men

of Jarrow isn't the march I should like best
to see and which I think would do most
good.

The people I really want to see march are the
members of Parliament, with the Premier and his
Cabinet at their head.

I should like to see them marching through
Durham to Jarrow and Tyneside; I should like
to see them marching in South Wales.

Then, perhaps, the problem of the "special
areas" would be tackled in earnest.

Apart from the members who themselves
represent constituencies in these unhappy districts,
Parliament has only the vaguest knowledge of
their plight.

Prosperity is returning; trade and employment
figures get steadily better and better; it is assumed
that things must be improving in the special areas
as well.

Members of Parliament who know the facts
protest against this easy optimism, but they are
dismissed as publicity hunters, trying to curry
favour with their constituents.

Anyhow, have not Ministers got the matter in
hand?

These comforting delusions would not survive
for long if Parliament marched to Jarrow. And
I believe that if our M.P.s actually saw for themselves the blighted towns and villages of the special
areas, looked into the pinched, pale faces of their
men and women and little children, went into

their homes and learned how they live, action would come swiftly.

But Parliament won't make this voyage of discovery. It won't go to Jarrow. So Jarrow must come to Westminster.

These marches, we are told, can do no good. I admit at once that there are some marches of which it is difficult to approve. They are organized by those who hope to make political capital out of misery and distress—they are carried out in a spirit of hatred.

But even such marches as these may stir our conscience—may help to bring home to us, in our comfortable complacency, the plight of the "forgotten men" who, in our country no less than in America, are a challenge to statesmanship—and to Christianity.

There is no hatred behind this Jarrow Pilgrimage. There is no question of suffering being exploited for selfish ends or partisan advantage. It is not a demonstration by a class; it is an appeal by a community, the expression, in the words of the Archdeacon of Northumberland, of "a community's deep sense of frustration and despair."

Indeed, we may say that the marchers represent not only Jarrow, but all those places which still lie derelict in spite of the return of prosperity elsewhere.

It is well that we should be reminded that there are such places where still no wheel turns, no

chimney smokes, and the sound of the hammer is
silent. It is well that the fact of this continuing
unemployment, with all that it means in waste
of life and of life's possibilities, should be brought
home to us.

We live far too much in our own little group.
The things and the people we see are the things
and the people that are real to us.

Distress on the doorstep demands and receives
our attention, while distress at a distance doesn't
seem so terrible. We have for the populations of
the depressed areas the same vague benevolence
that we have for the people in China and Africa,
about whom missionaries occasionally talk to us.
We wish them well, but it isn't our job to do
anything about it.

To all who have talked to any of the Jarrow
marchers, who have attended one of their
meetings, or who have seen them pass, these dim
and far-away shadows have been clothed with
flesh and blood, have been brought near.

I am glad of that. Britain is a whole, not just
a collection of separate districts or parts. And
Britain cannot be truly healthy, cannot justly
pride herself on weathering the storm of the slump
while these depressed areas remain.

I had meant so say something also of the blind
marchers who are demonstrating in Trafalgar
Square. They represent yet another community
—a community scattered throughout the land,
but made one by a common affliction.

Here, again, a march to London brings home to

us, with dramatic force and power, problems we
are apt to ignore, because they do not happen
to be our own. But here, also, we have a duty.

I have met many sightless people.   I have
visited the depressed areas.   I have talked with
men who, by no fault of their own, have been out
of work for years.

One of the things they find hardest of all to bear
is the sense of isolation, the feeling that they are
cut off from the general body of the people, that
they have been forgotten, that no one cares what
becomes of them.

These marches are an effort to overcome that.
The marchers are saying in effect: "We are men
of the same blood and bone as yourselves. What
are you going to do about us?"

Woe to us if all that we answer is: "Am I my
brother's keeper?"

The man who said that was a murderer.

I HAVE recently been, for four days, to Burn-ham-on-Sea, and except that I couldn't play golf on the course I like best, and that I was given the difficult task of spotting the winning child at a fancy dress children's carnival, I had a very good time.

While I was still in Somerset I read of the scheme to preserve Glastonbury Tor, some miles away, as one of the properties of the National Trust. I read of new Glastonbury pilgrimages. And my thoughts went to the most wonderful little town in our land.

Some of you doubtless have passed through its streets and paused to admire the carved stone front of the ancient pilgrims' inn. You may even have gone on pilgrimage to the abbey. To many, however, it will be only a name, or perhaps its very name will be unknown. Yet it is the most important name in our history—for Glastonbury is the cradle of Christianity in England.

You may still see, in the abbey grounds, the site of the wattle-roofed church which was our first Christian place of worship. Here was lit a lamp that has never since gone out—and all the great cathedrals, Canterbury and St. Paul's, Salisbury and Wells, Winchester and York Minster, all the Christian churches from Land's End to the Border, are daughter churches of Glastonbury.

When St. Augustine landed on our shores, in this one place Christianity was already established. He found here an island of faith in the midst of paganism.

It produced St. Dunstan, Abbot of Glastonbury and Archbishop of Canterbury, who first dreamed of a united England, untroubled by the fierce rivalries of local chieftains, and made his dream come true when, close on a thousand years ago, he crowned Edgar King of All England at Bath.

So, in the cradle of our English Christianity, down centuries that elsewhere were filled with strife, peace went hand in hand with faith.

It was a place of reconciliation. Here, according to a tradition older than Malory's story of the enchanted waters, is the burial place of King Arthur and Guinevere.

And every year, on Weary-all Hill, the Holy Thorn blossomed on Christmas Day, in token of God's mercy.

Have you heard the tradition of the Holy Thorn? In the darkest hour of Christianity, when Our Lord hung on the Cross and the hopes of His disciples seemed quenched in blood and faith a mockery, it is said that one man—Joseph of Arimathea—dared to avow himself a Christian. Pilate allowed him to take down the body of

Jesus from the tree—and he laid it, reverently, in the tomb that he had prepared for himself.

There followed the miracle of the Resurrection.

But St. Joseph's tale does not end there. Throughout the Middle Ages, not only England, but all Christendom believed that, leaving Palestine with eleven companions, Joseph wandered far and wide until at last he came to Glastonbury, then an island.

He landed on Weary-all Hill and, knowing that now his odyssey was at an end, thrust his staff into the ground, where the dry wood broke into bud and blossom.

Thus was planted the Holy Thorn, cuttings of which still survive at Glastonbury.

Merely legend, you tell me. And perhaps you add that you don't believe the bit about King Arthur either.

Perhaps it is. I won't argue with you about it. But, fact or fancy, a legend may enshrine a profound spiritual truth.

With him to Glastonbury, it is said, St. Joseph brought the Holy Grail, the chalice from which our Lord drank at the Last Supper. And the most famous of all the episodes of the Arthurian saga, those which have inspired most surely poets and painters, are the ones which deal with the Quest of the Grail.

In a sense, are not all of us who are Christians engaged upon that quest?

We set ourselves a goal we shall never in life

attain, dream of a perfection we shall never see. However strongly we press on towards the mark it seems constantly to recede from us.

But we trust that our striving is not vain.

And we know that, without our dream and our striving, life would be void of beauty and death would be robbed of hope.

The ruined church on Glastonbury Tor points, a finger of stone, to Heaven. The bare walls of the ancient abbeys speak to us of an age when God, perhaps, was nearer to men than He sometimes seems to-day.

But God is the same from generation to generation. It is we who have changed. We have withdrawn ourselves from Him, not He from us.

And once more the winds of God are stirring the dry leaves of the world. Perhaps the revival of religion as a living force in the hearts of all men is nearer than we think.

WHY KINDNESS TO DOGS, CRUELTY TO DEER?

THE average Briton prides himself on being kind to animals. Certainly any form of cruelty to a dog or a cat, or a horse moves him to generous indignation.

It is strange—and in some ways hopeful—that this feeling, which seems almost instinctive, is of comparatively recent growth.

Naturally enough, it was on those animals which stand in close relationship to man that the first reformers concentrated.

But as time went on an increasing number of people began to ask themselves whether that was enough.

They saw men and women, who were kind to their horses and dogs, taking part in sports which seemed to involve considerable cruelty.

Why, asked these new reformers, condemn some forms of cruelty to animals, and condone others? Surely the thing that matters is the suffering, not the kind of animal that is made to endure it?

"Blood sports" have been part of English life for centuries. It is not easy to see evil in something to which we have been accustomed since childhood, and which has the sanction of a long tradition.

Well, traditions may be bad as well as good. They represent inherited error just as often as inherited truth. And it is the reformer's job to attack and clear away whatever is harmful in them.

To-morrow the members of the National Trust are being asked to declare that, in view of the cruelties it involves, hunting and shooting for sport should be prohibited on Trust lands.

The National Trust owns a large number of our most celebrated beauty-spots. It holds them on trust for the nation. If it imposes this ban, the moral effect will be tremendous.

To me, the question of blood sports is a simple one. Am I entitled for my own pleasure to inflict suffering on an animal?

If he stops to think about it, can any decent man take part in such a "sport" as stag-hunting, which will very shortly be beginning again on Exmoor? There is mental, as well as physical, cruelty in stag-hunting.

I am aware that, in some hunts, deer are despatched with a gun, but even if the "kill" is quickly over there has been all the agony of the long pursuit.

Some time ago, a well-known business man and sportsman who, in his own words, had "experienced brutalities in many forms", sent me a report from a newspaper.

A stag, fleeing from the hounds, came, wild-eyed and panting, into the streets of a country town.

The sight of it seemed to awaken the strange hysteria of the hunt in a crowd of men.

The terrified animal was chased into a garden, where it was held to await the arrival of the huntsmen.

The newspaper spoke of frightened women and children looking on at the brutal scene. What must the children, taught at school to be kind to animals, have thought of it?

My correspondent was outspoken in his comments on this harrying of an inoffensive and beautiful creature. To him the sport in which such happenings were possible was cruel and cowardly. He wanted to protest against it. He wanted to stop it.

He didn't mind "brutal fights"—so long as they were fair fights. But he had always demanded "an even break for both sides."

And he didn't find it in stag-hunting.

Don't tell me, please, that if stag-hunting were abolished the deer would be exterminated.

Better that than to preserve them to be tortured!

But the deer needn't be exterminated. There is room on Exmoor—and elsewhere—for deer reserves.

If the herds become too numerous they can be thinned out by humane means. There are no insuperable difficulties in the way.

That, indeed, is what will probably be done in

the National Trust properties if the ban on hunting and shooting is carried.

I have concentrated on stag-hunting here because it seems to me the most abominable of all the blood sports. I cannot understand why the Bill for its suppression, prepared by the R.S.P.C.A. and introduced in the House of Commons by Mr. J. A. Lovat-Fraser seven years ago, was allowed to drop.

Every day Parliament begins its proceedings with prayer. If our M.P.'s would think back to their schooldays, and to those lines of Coleridge that doubtless they then learned by heart——

He prayeth best who loveth best
All things both great and small;
For the dear God who loveth us,
He made and loveth all.

—I think they might feel that daily prayer a mockery until they had ended for ever the tragedy of the hunted stag—and the hunted hind.

"IF only I could know what was going to happen. If only I could be sure!"

We've all said that—or thought it—at some time or other. And because of this universal, very natural, and very human desire there have always been fortune-tellers.

We cross the gypsy's hand with silver, and if the fee is large enough, or there seems a possibility of further business, the gypsy tells us what she thinks we want to hear.

It's very profitable for the gypsy—and there are times when it's very pleasant, very consoling, and very flattering to her clients.

But there are other times when it is harmful and dangerous.

A girl—or a man—consults a palmist or a crystal-gazer "just for fun." It isn't done seriously. There are jokes about it afterwards.

But perhaps something is said that comes near the mark—something about the past of which the fortune-teller couldn't have any real knowledge, or that seems to confirm some vague idea of the client's. If this one point is right, may not others be right too? Perhaps there is something in it after all. So the dupe argues.

And, in spite of all professions of indifference or disbelief, the prophecies are remembered.

Well, there is something in it. The fortune-teller is a charlatan—but no charlatan can ever be successful without a certain native shrewdness.

And long experience gives a superficial knowledge of character.

The palmist, for instance, does not merely read her client's hands. She reads their faces also. And she listens as well as talks.

Unconsciously, many of the people who consult fortune-tellers tell them a great deal.

And they don't know they are doing it—so that the knowledge and insight of the clever humbug who takes advantage of their simplicity seem wonderful to them.

The fortune-teller mentions a tall, blond man with blue eyes. It is a shot in the dark. But it is a fairly safe one. Most people do know some one who can be so described.

Apparently, in this case, it has scored a bull. "That will be Jack," says the woman who wants to peep into the future. She doesn't realize how she is playing into the fortune-teller's hands.

It may be that all the materials thus presented to the fortune-teller and all the hints she receives from her study of her client are used with a measure of discretion, and that the fortune is innocuous enough.

But this is not always the case. Sometimes

statements are made that can only be ascribed to wanton mischief.

The fortune-teller plays on her client's fears and suspicions, her vanities and weaknesses in a way that is absolutely criminal. A wife lets slip a hint of jealousy. The fortune-teller seizes upon it, suggests that the husband needs watching, or that one of the wife's friends is trying to steal him.

There is a dark-haired woman. Or is it a blonde? Beware of the dark-haired woman—or the blonde. Don't trust her.

And those nights when her husband says he is late at the office.

A young woman comes in, discontent and restlessness stamped on her pretty face, marring what would otherwise be charming. She is wearing a wedding ring.

Here is a girl, accustomed to go out to shop, or office, or factory, who has suddenly found herself cooped up in a tiny flat or council cottage, with not enough work to keep her occupied, and no one to speak to. She is finding life desperately dull. And things aren't much better when her husband comes home. She wants to go out—to visit the local picture house, or to dance. He is tired and wants to stay at home. "What's the good of a home if you're never in it?"

Probably, in any case, there is no money, or very little money, for amusements.

They're still paying for their furniture. The rise he expected hasn't materialized. She isn't a very good manager, and household bills are proving a problem.

Unscrupulously the fortune-teller exploits the young wife's discontent, her boredom, her desire for life and movement and colour.

She suggests adventure. There is a man—young, handsome, rich—waiting to give her all the things she craves for. They are hers for the taking. And she needn't be afraid.

"I see two husbands in your hand. You will marry again. A much better marriage."

How many pitiful stories of sin and shame, sobbed out in a parson's study, have had some such beginning as this! I know that these women are foolish. But they would probably have won through to usefulness and contentment but for the poisonous suggestions made to them.

The harpies who, in either of these ways, unsettle homes for gain have much to answer for. The marriage may, indeed, be saved from shipwreck—but too often something that was precious has been shattered. It is "never glad, confident morning again."

I wish that its victims could be made to realize how false and wicked fortune-telling is—and how heavy a price may have to be paid for these unworthy suspicions and feverish excitements.

There are times too when the palmist or clairvoyant prophesies disease—or even death.

And upon the superstitious mind fear rolls down like a cloud, blotting out the sunlight.

We cannot escape fear. Every gain is haunted by the shadows of loss.

Over the most perfect human love there hangs the foreboding of mortality. The joys of parenthood are interwoven inextricably with sharp anxieties.

But here an old crone's malice, or reckless, irresponsible guess, gives a new edge to fear— and turns, perhaps, a wife or mother's apprehensions into blind unreasoning terror.

Those who regard fortune-telling with amused tolerant contempt are wrong. It is an evil, a cancer, that should be fought and destroyed.

And I must confess that I cannot understand those who allow any form of it to be practised at church fairs or fêtes, or in aid of any charity.

I willingly admit that those who give their services voluntarily on such occasions are, as a rule, both careful and discreet. But the presence of such "attractions" on these occasions lends countenance to other forms of fortune-telling that are not innocuous.

People argue: "What is right at the church fair at home cannot be wrong at the seaside." The amateur paves the way for the professional.

Or perhaps an hour's "innocent amusement" with a planchette in a laughing circle of friends leads to solitary attempts to pierce the future with the aid of the same fantastic folly.

That way, sometimes, madness lies.

Fortune-telling is a fraud, and often a wicked fraud.

The future is not fixed. We cannot foretell or foresee it. All that we can do is to work, honestly and lovingly, in the present for the good that we desire—and to pray for faith so that, whatever may befall us, we shall meet it with a stout heart.

We may endure hardness, we may go down into deep waters of grief, our dearest dreams may come to nothing or, realized, may turn to dust and ashes in the mouth.

But if we have faith we know that evil must be overcome at the last, "that all things work together for good to them that love God."

There are occasions, perhaps, when we find that difficult to believe, when doubt overwhelms us, and the way seems dark. But, if we ask Him, God will give us strength in our hour of need.

The future is in His hands. All we need know of it is that He will not fail us. And, in His own good time, He will bring us home.

THE other day I was reading a book of memoirs in which a certain person was described as a "good sport."

He had subscribed to a pet charity of the author's at a time when he was heavily in debt. A little later he found himself in the bankruptcy court.

It is easy to gain a reputation for generosity if we open our pockets to everybody except our creditors. I could be a "good sport," too. I could sit down and write out cheques for half a dozen deserving charities to which I've never been able to give as much as I wanted.

The cheques would be gratefully received. The money would undoubtedly do good. But— I wouldn't be paying it. The real—unacknowledged, unwilling—benefactors of these charities would be the tradesmen who would have to wait for payment of their accounts till my bank balance recovered.

There is nothing spectacular about paying our way—settling bills promptly, living within our income all the time.

There is something richly satisfying about

making a splash with a chequebook or a pocket-book—handing out subscriptions to this and that or standing drinks all round.

But, however much we may like that particular sort of limelight, we have no right to buy it with other people's money. That's what we are doing when we let bills accumulate and use the cash that should have paid them for self-glorification.

It may seem a dashing thing to do. We may "kid ourselves" that we can use the money so much better than the "poor fish" to whom we owe it. Many of us have a sneaking fancy for the rôle of Robin Hood, who took from the rich to give to the poor.

Well, there is a lot to be said for separating a millionaire from part of his millions and giving it to a hospital. But it is far better for the separation to be a willing one. It does more good to the millionaire. And the hospital gets more money.

Anyway, I'm afraid that the only millionaires in the shopkeeping line work on a "strictly cash" basis. The tradesmen who let accounts run on are, as a rule, those who are hardest put to it to obtain a bare living.

Shopkeepers may be "dull dogs." They may be "money-grabbers." But don't we grab our own pay envelopes or salary cheques hard enough?

And wouldn't we shout the place down if they weren't forthcoming at the proper time?

I know we have worked for what we get. But the shopkeeper has worked for his money too.

He has given us service. And in letting us have goods on credit he has lent us part of his savings.

We would look pretty blue if our employer expected us to do that—if he made it a condition of our getting or keeping our job.

But isn't that just what we do to the shop-keeper when we say to him: "If you don't give us credit, there are other shops that will?"

These are points to bear in mind if ever we are tempted to "let the tradesmen wait" so that we can make a bit of a splash, win the reputation of being a "good sport."

But there is another kind of "good sport." He's the man who makes his wife and family pay for his popularity. They go without all sorts of things they need so that he may have plenty to spend.

He thinks he is a real sportsman because he goes to the dog races twice a week. He always has money to back his fancy. He always has money for a football pool. He always has money for a drink. If his luck is in he is generous. The round is on him. Even when he is not so fortunate, he will still go on spending. Possibly he will bor-row a bit till pay day.

I do not suggest that everybody who goes to dog races, or has an occasional "flutter," or fills in a football pool coupon, is like this.

There are innumerable people who do these things who are still good husbands and fathers, who never spend or risk more than they can afford.

I may think they are foolish—there are better

things a man can do with his pocket money—
but I don't condemn them.

Life is a drab affair for millions, and I can
understand the temptation that a "little flutter"
offers.

But there are too many men who gamble on
the "heads I win, tails the wife loses" principle.

They spend all their winnings, and their losses
come out of the housekeeping money. They will
even pawn all that there is pawnable in the home
in order to go on gambling.

I've known many cases of this kind. And of
practically every one I've heard it said by someone, "——is a good chap, really. He hurts
nobody but himself."

It isn't true. No married man can behave like
this and hurt nobody but himself. His wife and
children suffer far more than he does.

And in nine cases out of ten the single man who
is this kind of fool is also making other people
miserable.

There may be a girl who is in love with him.
Or he lives at home with his mother—and she
goes through all that his wife would have to bear,
if he had one.

Perhaps she goes through more—for a mother
will often stand from a son what no wife would
stand from her husband.

Curious, isn't it, that we should call people like
these "good sports"?

4

For what do we mean by the phrase? I asked the question of a man who had used it. He replied: "A good sport is a man who plays the game."

Is the gambler or boon companion whose home is stripped bare and whose wife and children often haven't enough to eat playing the game? Is the man who makes a habit of bilking tradesmen playing the game? Is the man who is generous at his creditors' expense playing the game?

The greatest game of all is the game of Life. And what counts in that game is not what we do and what we are in the public house or on the dog track, but what we do and are at our work, in our homes, in our relations with other people who, in one way or another, depend on our honesty and good faith.

It is not of these things that we think when we talk of a man being a "good sport." I know that.

But which is more worth while, which would you rather be—the "good sport" of the pub or the betting ring, or a good son, a good husband, a good father, a good neighbour?

THE other day a man came to me in great trouble. He had put ten shillings on a horse he'd been told was a "certainty"—and had lost.

That was bad enough—ten shillings meant a lot in that man's home.

But there was worse to come. The money he had lost wasn't his own. He had "borrowed" it from the till. And if it wasn't replaced at once he might lose his job—might even be given in charge as a thief. He was in tears as he told the pitiful story.

Now, he wasn't a boy. He didn't have that excuse to offer. He didn't, in fact, try to offer any excuse.

But I knew something of his life. I knew he was hard-working, decent, sober, a good husband and father, and—in spite of the ten shillings—honest.

He had been all these things before he "borrowed" that unlucky ten bob. He was still all these things after it.

One lapse doesn't make a criminal. No one who has any sympathetic understanding of human nature will condemn a man for a single false step.

Nor would any one who stopped to think read

him a long lecture on dishonesty—and end by
saying that he must go back to his employer and
confess what he had done. Or deliver a homily
on gambling—and come to the same conclusion.

I hate dishonesty. I have seen too much of the
suffering that is caused by betting to try to defend
it. But—it isn't only the poor who gamble.

From time to time you find earnest people
attacking fiercely the great social evil of gambling.
They tell you of enormous sums spent on postal
orders for football pool promoters, of men and
women who will pawn even their furniture to
back a horse.

But let Lord Tom Noddy say he has just lost
five hundred pounds on the Stock Exchange and
they are all sympathy. Or how he won five
hundred pounds on the Stock Exchange and they
are all admiration.

They may even ask if he can recommend a
promising investment, just as a workman asks a
"knowledgeable" mate if he can put him on to a
good thing.

It isn't an investment they want any more than
the workman does. It's a gamble. They are both
looking for "something for nothing."

Well, I don't believe that what is essentially the
same thing can be legitimate in the case of the
rich and the reverse in the case of the poor.

Let us be honest about this social evil.
Buying stocks and shares, or any sort of produce

or commodity, in the hope of a rise in price, is as much gambling as betting on a horse, or a dog, or a football team.

And what's the difference between playing contract for money—"just a small stake, to give interest to the game"—and the workman's nap, or rummy, or even crown and anchor?

There is, of course, one unanswerable argument. No one has a right to gamble with money that is required to feed and clothe his children, or to pay the rent or the instalments on the furniture.

No one has a right to reduce his family to penury and destitution so that he may have the excitement of a "flutter."

I've seen a gambler's home stripped bare of almost every stick of furniture and with nothing in the larder.

But I've seen other homes reduced to exactly the same ghastly state—not by gambling, but by drink. And the gambler doesn't, as a rule, knock his wife and children about as the drunkard very often does.

I've also known cases where hundreds of families have been reduced to poverty because their bread-winners were employed by men who gambled, not on the racecourse, not on the Stock Exchange, but in their own business.

In the end they had to put up the shutters—and their workpeople were out of a job.

But I'm not going to say, because some men are drunkards, that every one who drinks a glass of beer is wicked. And I know that in business there must always be an element of risk.

Does this mean that there is nothing we can do about gambling—that we must just sit, with arms folded, and let it go on, careless of what misery it causes?

I don't think so.

But let us recognize that, so long as we ourselves gamble, no matter what form our gambling takes, we aren't going to carry conviction when we tell the man who has a bob each way on a horse, or fills up his weekly football coupon, that it is wicked to bet.

If we want to stamp out gambling entirely, we must start by giving it up ourselves.

If we're not prepared to do that, if we're determined to go on, for example, backing our fancy in rubber shares, we've no right to interfere with other people's football pools.

But there are some, perhaps, who don't gamble and who are entitled to say something on the subject. They might, I suggest, say something like this:—

"Have your flutter if you must, so long as it's only yourself who loses. You're really being rather foolish because even if you win now and again and your winnings look pretty good to you, practically every one who bets loses in the long run. And there's a lot of more useful ways of spending money. However, that's your affair.

"But don't gamble with the money that should

be keeping the home going, or with the savings that are meant to tide the family over a possible lean period later on. You've no right to buy your excitement at the expense of the wife and kids."

Every one, surely, must admit the fairness of that.

And I believe that, tackling the question in this way, we are far more likely to create a public opinion hostile to the gambling that breaks up homes than if we denounce all gambling as a sin.

That isn't compromising with the Devil. There's a difference—an enormous difference—between the man who is wicked and the man who is merely foolish.

All gambling is folly. But there is some gambling that is wickedness. It is only right that we should make a distinction between the two.

And it's not among those who back horses or bet on football results that we find the wickedest gambling of all. Nor is it on the Stock Exchange.

There are people who gamble with lives.

They may neglect safety measures in coal-mine or factory to obtain a bigger output, hoping that nothing will go wrong.

Or they may send a ship to sea overloaded and under-manned.

Or they may take chances driving a car or a motor-cycle on the highway.

Or, placed in positions of power and authority,

they may play a game of bluff with the statesmen of other countries, incurring the risk of war, with all that war may mean.

While gamblers like these continue, we're rather wasting our time when we worry over-much about football pools.

DIVORCE

I HAVE been asked two questions on a subject which concerns vitally both Church and State.

Would I remarry a divorced person?

Would I give the Sacrament to a divorced person who had remarried?

The answer in both cases is "yes."

I do not like divorce. I believe in the sacred character of the marriage tie.

But there are certain unions which have lost their sanctity, which can never realize the aim and purpose of Christian marriage. They are a mockery of holy wedlock.

There is no virtue in the form without the spirit. It can never be a Christian duty to perpetuate a lie, or to condemn the innocent to lifelong misery and degradation, or to deny them a second chance of happiness when, through no fault of their own, a first marriage has ended in disaster.

Even if there had been faults, is it our part to judge? The Church must rebuke sin. But it also proclaims forgiveness. Its ministers are charged to call sinners to repentance, not to thrust them into hell. A loveless marriage is a hell on earth. Loneliness can be hell. Sin makes its own hell always.

And, let me add, sin can exist within the circle of marriage as well as outside it. No form of words recited by a parson can hallow brutality and lust. The marriage service does not make a woman the property of her husband or absolve him from the obligations of decency and respect.

Yet I have known cases—as has every parson of experience—where men have treated their wives as they would not have dared to treat a common harlot. All too often the strains of the "Wedding March" are the prelude to something approaching outrage.

What is the use of telling the victims of this legalized lust that marriage is a sacrament?

I believe that the Church has made a profound mistake in its attitude to holy matrimony.

It has attached undue importance to rites and ceremonies and not enough to the spirit, which alone can give them significance.

The essence of the marriage service is surely that two people, wishing to go hand in hand through life and to establish a home and family, take vows of mutual love, mutual fidelity, and mutual respect, and ask God's blessing on their purpose.

Christian marriage is the keeping of these vows, the building-up of a life together that will be pleasing in the sight of God. It is a partnership of equals—or it is nothing.

If the vows are broken, if the happy relationship of love and confidence is destroyed and cannot be re-established, if the home becomes a hell, or if one partner repudiates his responsibilities and leaves the other to face life alone, there is no Christian marriage. To pretend that there is does not uphold an ideal, nor does it endanger an ideal to smash the shell from which the substance has departed.

In certain circumstances, therefore, I believe that divorce may be legitimate. Nor would I deny the sacraments of the Church to those who, having secured a divorce, find love and happiness, the realities of Christian marriage, with a new partner.

I recall one case in which, after a disastrous first marriage with a woman of loose character a man married again. He is happy in this second marriage. Children have been born to his wife and himself and are being brought up in an atmosphere of love and confidence.

That man regularly receives Holy Communion. His parson would not dream of denying it to him. But there are other clergymen of the Church of England who would say to him: "Your first wife is still alive. Therefore, although a court of law has granted you a divorce, the Church regards you as an adulterer. You are living in sin. Unless you separate from your wife, you cannot communicate."

These parsons seek to break up homes in the name of Christ. They would condemn men and women who love each other to lives of loneliness, and refuse to children a father's care and guidance.

I cannot believe that this cold inhumanity is in accordance with the will of God. It is utterly alien to all that Our Lord did and said on earth, to the whole spirit of His mission.

Personally, I would give Communion to any one who asked for it in a reverent spirit and with a desire to do better. It is not mine to withhold.

It is a service for sinners as well as saints. I would not deny it to a murderer who wished to make his peace with God. Who would?

Shall we show less compassion, less human sympathy, to those unfortunates who have been caught in the net of an unhappy marriage and cut themselves free, than we do to the poisoner?

That, briefly, is my attitude, and the attitude which I would like the Church to take, to those who have been divorced and remarried. But I freely admit that any extension or widening of the grounds for divorce calls for anxious care and consideration.

This is not a matter on which the Church of Christ can accept whatever standards are established and enacted by the State. It must apply to all legislation on the subject the test of Christian principles.

For example, all Christian people will denounce, and denounce passionately, that heartless and damnable decree of the Nazis, which permits a German to put away his wife for no other reason than that she is a Jewess. Nor can we acquiesce in the laws of certain American States, which make it easier to change one's wife or one's husband than to change one's house, or the furniture that house contains.

It has been suggested that the new Marriage Act, is the thin end of the wedge of the Americanization of our divorce law. I can see no justification for that charge.

I see no threat to Christian marriage in this Act. On the contrary, I think that it will strengthen Christian marriage.

One of its clauses makes it impossible to petition for divorce until a marriage has lasted some years. This may prove some check upon hasty and injudicious marriage.

It also gives young married people a chance to settle down; to adjust themselves to a relationship which, in the first few months, often presents unexpected difficulties; to learn the art of living together.

I am told that, in the view of lawyers of experience, another clause should be effective in ending the scandal of collusive divorce.

Desertion for so many years; cruelty, and insanity which remains incurable after so many years' confinement, are made grounds for divorce. Surely there is nothing here to offend the conscience of Christian people. The marriage has, in fact, ceased to exist.

No one need petition for divorce in these or any other circumstances. But we cannot, in common humanity, deny to those who wish it that second chance which the Act gives them.

The Act also provides that, if a judicial separation order has been in force for some years, the person who obtained it may be granted a divorce.

This is a valuable reform. In thousands of cases these orders have led to irregular unions.

Some of these unions approach far more nearly to the ideals of Christian marriage than many which have been solemnized in church. They have not been entered upon lightly. They will be ended only by death.

But they are poisoned by the knowledge that, under the existing law, the marriage which both partners desire may be forever impossible, and that they must either be denied the gift of children, or that any children who are born must bear the stigma of illegitimacy.

I do not seek, in writing thus, to palliate sin. But those who opposed the Marriage Bill would condemn such sinners to continue in their sin. Or perhaps invite them to commit a sin far more flagrant.

What are we to say of the man who, having lived with a woman in an irregular union throughout the years of her prime, abandons her as age begins to lay its hand upon her? Are we to welcome him as a repentant sinner?

I think I can guess what Christ would have said to such a man. But He told us that to those who loved much, much might be forgiven.

There is one serious defect in the Act. The

conciliation proposals which it originally contained have been dropped.

That is a point on which the Church ought to make its voice heard.

So long as there is any possibility of reconciliation, no marriage should be dissolved until a real effort has been made to save it.

In my view it is by concentrating on this and by proclaiming, in unmistakable accents, what Christian marriage may and ought to be, that the Church will best express the mind of Our Lord.

To deny the Sacrament to men and women who are trying to lead decent lives, to oppose reforms in the civil divorce law which commend themselves alike to compassion and common sense, is to choose the way of the Pharisees rather than the way of Christ.

But I think that perhaps there might be a different form of service—not necessarily a second-rate or second-best form—for those who, having married and been divorced, seek to be remarried in church. It is not fair to a parson to have to say the same words at the second marriage as, perhaps, he has already said at the first.

Meanwhile, I believe that Christian people may view the Act with a good conscience. Would to God that all the social legislation of our Parliament were inspired by a similar feeling for human suffering and an equal compassion and good will.

YOU remember the old joke about the lion-tamer who could overawe the fiercest of wild animals with a single glance and who went in terror of the little slip of a woman who was his wife?

It was always a good joke. Not because there is anything particularly funny in a man being scared of his wife, but because we're all afraid of something.

So, when we laugh at the lion-tamer we are really, in a sense, laughing at ourselves—trying to convince ourselves that our own fears are groundless and unreasonable.

But fear isn't exorcised so easily. It is too deeply rooted.

It is one of the first emotions we experience on coming into the world. The baby is afraid—desperately afraid—of falling. That is why it cries when any one holds it who isn't accustomed to infants.

That fear never quite leaves us. Have you ever dreamed of falling through space? It is one of the most disconcerting of nightmares.

You awaken from it weak and trembling, hardly able to believe that, after all, you are really safe in bed.

As life goes on, fears multiply. They are, perhaps, foolish and unnecessary. That doesn't make them any the less real.

It's no good saying to a child who is afraid of the dark: "There's nothing to be frightened at." The child *is* frightened. Imagination peoples the dark with menace. It will go on doing so in spite of your reassurances. You can't reason with a child that is afraid. For fear goes deeper than reason.

Even now, perhaps, you are sometimes afraid of the dark yourself. A woman told me recently that, whenever she was alone in the house, she put on all the lights.

"I know it's silly," she said, "but I daren't even turn off the hall light when I go upstairs to bed."

Scientists sometimes explain this by what they call "ancestral memory." To primitive man night was full of perils. And we have spoken for centuries of "The Powers of Darkness."

All these things have a cumulative effect. Suggestion and tradition reinforce instinct. Besides, we feel helpless in the dark.

The sense of helplessness is at the root of most of our fears.

I don't know what your particular fear is. There are so many different types of fear abroad in the world to-day.

There are probably more people afraid of losing their jobs than ever before. There are always people who are afraid of illness.

5

Every one who thinks at all about world affairs is to-day desperately afraid of war. I heard the other day of a woman who, during the last year or so, has been reliving in her dreams the air-raid experiences of her youth. She can't understand why, after a long interval, these dreams should be recurring. But I think I can guess the reason.

There is a long catalogue of what doctors call neurotic fears. Many men and women are scared of any sort of responsibility.

They won't undertake any job in which they have to think and decide for themselves. Or, if they do attempt it, they have a nervous break-down.

Thousands are afraid of marriage.

Whatever form our fear may take, if we face it, if we dig down to its roots, we discover that what we are really afraid of is ourselves.

We are afraid of life because we do not feel equal to its demands. So often we run away from it. We refuse to accept responsibility.

We let others do our thinking and make our decisions. We turn our backs on marriage. We avoid the society of our fellow men and women, and shut ourselves up in a private world of dreams and fancies.

But to escape from life is not to escape from fear. The harder we run away, the harder the pursuing feet come after us.

Courage is just as much part of human nature as fear. And the highest courage of all is to do what you believe to be your duty, even if you are afraid.

I said that was the highest courage. But it isn't the rarest. There are countless people doing just that to-day. Some of them are working beside you; there are others in your family and among your friends.

We all know people like that. They don't think that they are doing anything very wonderful. But they are a perpetual inspiration.

You can be like them. Every step that you take to conquer your fear, or in spite of your fear, makes the next one easier.

Love, too, is as much one of the fundamental human emotions as fear. And love casts out fear.

What are you frightened of? Nothing that you cannot conquer; nothing that you cannot overcome.

You may be weak. We are all weak. But there are open to all of us sources of strength that are sufficient for all our needs.

There has been some argument recently as to the efficacy of prayer. The answer to prayer depends, I think, on what we ask for. But I have never yet known of any man or woman who has prayed, honestly and sincerely, for courage and strength to serve the purposes of life, and who has not received them.

God still helps us to help ourselves. While we travel the road of duty, He will travel with us, and in His strength we shall be strong.

A GIRL I have known since she was a child came to see me. She spoke about our disappointing summer, but I could see that wasn't really worrying her.

She mentioned one or two mutual acquaintances, and hardly listened to what I said in reply.

Then, abruptly, she plunged into the real business of the visit.

"I want you to help me," she said. "I want you to tell Tom and Mary"—she calls her father and mother by their Christian names, which aren't, by the way, Tom and Mary—"that they've just got to let me have a place of my own."

To her, as to thousands of other girls in like circumstances, a little flat, or even a room, so long as it's away from her people, represents freedom, independence.

It is a supreme ambition. And until it is realized I'm afraid that her parents' home won't be very peaceful.

I know how she feels. But there's another side to this subject.

Working in east-central and west London for a quarter of a century, I have learned something of the life of lonely women in London.

Some of those whom I have met there were comfortably off. They had good jobs or private incomes; their "one-woman" homes were cosy and cheerful.

But there were times when they all, even those who valued their "independence" most, felt desperately lonely and unhappy.

There were others—and they the majority—whose independence was made bitter by poverty. They had left youth behind and work was increasingly difficult to secure. If they did get a temporary job it was usually ill-paid.

I remember suggesting to a woman with private means, who had complained to me of the emptiness of her days, that she might try to help some of those others. I gave her a few addresses. She came back a day or two later.

"I've learned how lucky I am," she said. "At least I can be miserable in comfort."

She told me of the things she had seen. It was a tale of squalor and suffering—but a tale also of pitifully brave endeavour to give to tiny attic rooms or dark basements some touch of home.

"And the awful thing about it," she finished, "is that they're all scared of being thrown out. Living in places like that—and afraid of losing them! Starving themselves to pay rent for these foul dens!"

It is a continuing tragedy.

I have just been reading a pamphlet, "Consider

Her Palaces," issued by the Over Thirty Association, which has brought back, vividly and in detail, my memories of these lonely women and their struggle to keep their one miserable room.

I hope that every man who reads it will say to himself: "Suppose it were my sister who was living in these conditions, wouldn't I do something about it?"

Because I think that we must do something about it. The pamphlet is a challenge to the conscience of a Christian community—and a challenge which must be taken up.

The authoress, Miss Rosamond Tweedy, writes of bed-sitting rooms that "make one stand aghast to think that they are inhabited at all, and that people pay to live in them.

"I have seen," she continues, "a small ill-furnished ground-floor back room looking out on a blank wall, the walls sweating, and the paper peeling, the bed lumpy and doubtfully clean, with no bath, and conveniences which were totally inadequate. It was let at nine shillings a week."

These "bed-sits" are home to thousands of women—the only home they have.

The pamphlet doesn't say much about unemployment, but the annual report of the Over Thirty Association, which I have also in front of me, says a great deal.

It is harder to-day for a middle-aged woman to get permanent work than it was some years ago. And, as Miss Tweedy points out, even those women who are in work, if they belong to the lower-paid class of workers, when they look for a room to live in, usually have to "choose between hunger and squalor, and, in fact, often must suffer both."

A number of suggestions for tackling this problem are made. One of them is for one-room flatlets for lower-paid single workers, to be let at round about five shillings a week, subsidized from rates or taxes. Another is that meantime housing associations and trusts might provide such flatlets.

Personally, I should like to see the Church taking the lead in offering to those women struggling so bravely against fate, something more worthy of the name of home.

Undertaken to celebrate the centenary of their commission, that would give the "enthusiastical commissioners," as one old lady, their tenant, persisted in calling them, something to be enthusiastic about. But they are in a position of trusteeship, and any scheme they initiated would have to pay its way.

It might do so and still give these women infinitely better accommodation at rents no higher than they pay now.

Or, perhaps, some philanthropist, or group of philanthropists, might be willing to put up the capital cost, leaving the scheme to be run by the Ecclesiastical Commissioners. That would make the five shillings a week rental possible.

However it is done I suggest that there should

be, attached to each block of flatlets, a canteen and a club-room.

In the canteen, nourishing meals should be provided at cost. The club-room would, I hope, help to remove that soul-destroying loneliness which is the lot of so many of the women.

To-day our ears are more alert to the call of human need than at any previous period. But the women of whom I write are very largely inarticulate. They suffer in silence.

A MAN sat drinking in a public house. He had been drinking for a long time. He had swallowed considerable quantities of liquor. And as he drank he wept.

He wept because he had wasted his life. He wept because he had failed in his duty to his family. He wept because he had never appreciated his wife properly. He wept because his good intentions always went wrong.

But never mind. This time it would be different. Suddenly his mind glowed with a genial assurance of virtue. All, he resolved, would yet be well. He would redeem the past—make up for everything. He felt uplifted—noble.

Then the landlord said: "Time, gentlemen, please"—and he went home and swore at his wife.

I am reminded of that story—a story that has been true far too often—by certain religious celebrations, and the hope, expressed by earnest, well-meaning people, that they will launch a new "revival."

I distrust revivals and revivalist campaigns. They have sometimes the same effect on unbalanced minds as alcohol. They produce tears of penitence. They warm the soul. They make the good life seem easy. They give the illusion of virtue, of a special "election" by which the convert is set apart from other men.

But the repentance is as shortlived as the tears. The warmth rarely outlasts the final hymn. The decent life proves, next morning, just as hard, just as impossible and impracticable as it was before.

That is often the normal course of these emotional orgies. But there have been times when they have followed a darker path.

Men, "convicted" of sin, have taken their own lives in a frenzy of remorse. Hysterical women have lost the last remnants of sanity, found the mission hall the road to the asylum rather than the road to heaven. Children, forced to listen to lurid tales of hell-fire, have had their lives warped and twisted by terrors, of which all too often, they dare not speak.

True Christianity is not a stimulant. It is not a drug. It is not a bogy that fills the night with fear. It cannot be imposed from without. It is a growth, a flowering from the heart. It comes gently, almost unawares.

But it transforms the whole of life—as the spring flowers do the iron-bound earth. We may not talk much about it, but we try, however haltingly, to follow in the footsteps of Our Lord.

There is no sounding of trumpets to mark our

resolve; nor do we talk about past sins so that our present condition may shine brighter by contrast.

From time to time a "revival" passes over the country like a wave. Follow its course on the map and you will see how, almost always, it makes its greatest appeal, wins most converts, in those places where life is hardest, most uncertain.

And those who sing the revivalist hymns with the greatest fervour, who crowd the penitents' bench—are they not often the undernourished, those who have lived for years on the border-line of starvation?

Just as alcohol takes effect more quickly if one drinks on an empty stomach, so this intoxication of the emotions finds its natural prey among those who never have enough to eat.

Perhaps you think I am being too harsh. But where are the converts of past revival campaigns?

Are they leading Christian lives to-day?

Are they fighting for righteousness?

Did their conversion last?

It seems to me that we are too easily satisfied with names and phrases. We don't differentiate between the crude sentimentalities and bludgeoning threats of the revivalists and true Christianity.

Please don't misunderstand me. It is not the fault of the converts that their conversion doesn't endure. Nor do I question the sincerity of the revivalists.

What I do say is that too often the temporary success of a revival campaign is the measure of the failure of the Churches—and of professing Christians generally—to do their Christian duty.

If this were a Christian country in the full sense that phrase ought to bear, there would be no men and women so weakened by privation, living lives so drab and hopeless, as to be unable to withstand this assault on their emotions.

And if the Churches were the guardians of a living faith, and not, as too often happens, simply of a dead ritual, this caricature of religion would make little appeal.

So, in a double sense, I say that revivalism, as apart from true evangelism, can only flourish where Christianity has failed to take root.

Yet I find that, in the minds of a number of people, these revivals are regarded as a good thing; they may to-day even be represented as a response to the Archbishop of Canterbury's appeal for a "recall to religion."

It may be, of course, that the new revivals will avoid the errors and excesses of the old. I sincerely hope that they may, but I doubt it. Revivals all seem to follow the same pattern.

But perhaps this idea of revivalism as an answer to the Primate's call suggests a fundamental weakness in the whole "back-to-religion" campaign.

I have the greatest respect for the Archbishop. I want, as he does, to see religion made real to the millions of our people, becoming a force in all our hearts. But when he says, and others take up the cry, that we must get back to religion, I cannot help asking: "What religion?"

There is, in much that I have heard and read about the recall to religion, a suggestion that what is desired is a return to the formal observances of Victorian times. Organized religion is to be strengthened, re-established.

Personally, I think that the form is valueless without the spirit. There is no virtue in the Churches as Churches, but only in so far as they follow in the way of Our Lord.

How far are we prepared to do that?

Do we really want Christianity, with all that Christianity implies? Are we prepared to live in the spirit of Christ, not merely to render Him lip-service?

In short, are we prepared to make this land of ours really a Christian country?

Are we prepared to follow the teaching of Our Lord upon peace, and to follow it all the way?

Are we prepared to accept fully the Christian doctrine of our duty to our neighbours, and to act upon it in relation to the distressed areas and to all our economic and industrial problems?

Are we prepared to accept Christ's own definition of Christian duty, and not merely those parts of it which seem convenient and comfortable?

If we aren't so prepared, surely it would be

more honest to stop talking about a return to Christianity. What we really want might be described, much more accurately, as a return to convention.

But that opens up a big subject—too big for me to deal with now. Yet it is so important, so vital, that we should think straight about it, that we should know what we really want, that I propose to revert to it later.

Meanwhile, think it over for yourselves. What do we mean by religion? Is ours a fair-weather faith, or are we ready to make sacrifices for it?

Does "recall to religion" suggest to us a nation imbued with a passion for righteousness, or merely a nation resolved on respectability?

WICKEDNESS has gone out of fashion. Neither in fiction nor in real life are people bad any longer in the old whole-hogging way.

But it sometimes seems as if goodness has disappeared as well. We don't have contrasting black and white, only a uniform sombre grey.

Well, human nature has always been a strange mixture. But past generations had the courage of their sins—or of their virtues—in a way that we haven't.

They did things—good or evil—off their own bat. They accepted personal responsibility for all their actions.

To-day a great many of us are dodging that. We are trying to narrow down, as much as we can, the sphere in which we are directly answerable for what we do.

We can't, of course, evade personal responsibility completely. We must still stand on our own feet in our dealings with our family, our friends, and our neighbours.

If we break the law, and are found out, we must take the consequences.

But we live in an age of organization. And as members of an organization we sometimes do things which we should never dream of doing as individuals.

It is easier to be mean, or petty, or cruel, if we are acting in company with others. It is easier still when the victim is someone we don't know, who is merely a name on a works wages book or Case No. 199.

So we have the characteristic sin of the modern world—the sin of the committee-man.

We don't, as a rule, recognize it as a sin. It doesn't interfere with our appetite or keep us awake at night.

If, occasionally, we have qualms we shelter behind the decision of the committee or the board. "The committee says so-and-so." "The board has decided"—these familiar phrases help to cover up our personal responsibility.

Or we work to regulations laid down by some other board or committee higher up. "We can't go beyond the regulations," we say, and proceed to interpret them in a narrow and legalistic way.

We've become part of a machine—and we're dealing with men and women.

This evil—for it is an evil—extends into every department of modern life. It even poisons the springs of charity.

I'm not quite sure when the phrase "cold as charity" first came into common use, but I think it must have been about the time of the original charity committee.

There's no coldness in the right kind of personal

giving. It establishes a warm human relationship. And often the handshake, or the word of encouragement that goes with the material help, is the thing that counts most of all.

People who give in this way are sometimes "stung." But certain charity committees are so afraid of wasting their funds on the undeserving that those who most need—and most merit—assistance are either denied it altogether or suffer bitter humiliation before they get it.

I'm not saying that happens in every case. There are charity organizers who bring kindliness and human sympathy into impersonal giving.

But the big danger in our elaborately systematized benefactions is that we sometimes lose sight of the men and women and children we want to help in a mass of forms and statistics. The charity that is love is strangled by red tape.

All highly centralized organizations tend to go dead at the heart. There seems a curse of sterility on all G.H.Q.'s, whether in Church or State, business or charity.

Shut off from the current of common life, they issue their pompous edicts without ever trying to visualize what they will mean to the people affected by them.

Have you heard the story of the highly placed officer who, after the tragedy of Passchendaele had been going on for four months, motored out from general headquarters to visit the scene of operations for the first time?

As he saw the desolation of mud that was the

6

battlefield—and before he had reached the worst of the swamp—he burst into tears.

"Good God!" he cried. "Did we really send men to fight in that?"

That's how the G.H.Q.'s work, whatever kind of G.H.Q. they happen to be. Only, as a rule, those who thus work havoc with the lives of others don't see the results they have produced.

There seems to be some malevolent magic about Government departments, public authorities, and big official corporations.

It doesn't sour the milk of human kindness—it just bottles it up and shuts it away during office hours. The people in charge are working on paper, and all they need for that is ink.

That, at any rate, would seem the only possible explanation of such things as, among others, the continuing tragedy of the Special Areas, the way in which the means test has been permitted to break up family life, and the ironic spectacle of villages where farmers daren't sell surplus milk to their neighbours at a price they can afford, and babies and expectant mothers go without.

But nobody is personally responsible—it's always the board, or the committee, or the department.

An M.P. once told me how, when a Labour colleague had become a Cabinet Minister, he took along a deputation from the East End to see him.

Replying to the deputation, the Minister never used the word "I." It was "the Board" this and "the Board" that. At last my friend could stand it no longer. He broke in:—

"Steady, my friend. Try to remember the time when I was hanging on to the blooming Board's coat tails in Trafalgar Square, trying to keep it from talking treason!"

Now, that Minister was the best type of politician. He sacrificed his career for a principle. He is a humane and kindly man.

The truth is that, when we talk about the sin of the committee-man, we're talking about a sin we all share.

We may not be members of any board or committee ourselves, but we've helped to elect them, or some of them, and we are content to leave them to get on with it.

We've got the committee habit. We don't see evil and suffering as a challenge to ourselves. We see it as a problem for a committee or a board.

But evil and suffering will go on, the world will remain a place of heartbreak and tragedy for millions, until we all realize that we have a personal responsibility for putting at least our own little corner to rights.

We don't want committees to tinker with humanity's troubles or to create new ones. We want in our own hearts the faith that moves mountains, and the will to get on with the job of shifting them as *our* job, and no one else's.

Believe me, there are mountains enough—mountains of misery and wrong—for us to move.

The essential thing to remember is the wisdom

of the Founder of Christianity, who always suggested that people should think, not in terms of "cases" and "applicants" and "hands," but in terms of men, women and children.

WHENEVER religion is discussed nowadays, sooner or later you are bound to hear the phrase "empty pews."

I wish we parsons didn't talk quite so much about those empty pews. When we concentrate upon them, we get our problems in a false perspective.

We lose sight of the real task which confronts us.

That task is not to fill the empty pews. It is to fill the hearts of men and women with the love of God.

There may be a world of difference between the two.

The Churches are institutions. Those who love God and strive to follow in the way of Christ are a fellowship. The Churches have their creeds, their distinctive rites and observances.

Church membership denotes acceptance—qualified, perhaps, in some cases, but none the less real—of certain doctrines and ways of worship.

What Church we belong to may be a matter of accident rather than choice. Our membership may be merely formal and have little or no effect upon our lives.

75

But if we truly love God, all that we do takes on a new colour and a new significance. We dedicate ourselves to Him; we follow—we must follow—wherever He may lead us.

Probably He will lead us, not only to a new way of living, but also to some Church within which we may do useful work and, in any case, shall be able to join with others in praise and prayer.

But for the moment I'm going to ignore that side of it.

The question is how we are to win for Christianity those who are at present careless or indifferent, or even hostile.

Sometimes, as I have already indicated, newspaper articles may help.

I do not suggest, in saying this, that people are likely to be "converted" to Christianity by reading an article about religion.

But it may set some of them thinking. It may encourage them to lay their doubts and problems before someone who can help to solve them.

It may send them back to the New Testament.

I also believe that the open-air religious service —and the open-air meeting—can be of value.

Those summer holiday services on Blackpool sands, or at other popular seaside resorts, or at famous inland beauty-spots where hikers congregate reach many who never go to church in the ordinary way.

It may be idle curiosity that draws them to listen in the first place.

But perhaps—who knows?—some spoken word may bring back memories of childhood, of cleaner, happier days, and so prepare their hearts to receive the message of Our Lord.

The usefulness of the open-air religious meeting is of a different kind. It enables objections to Christianity, doubts about Christianity, to be crystallized in the form of questions.

People who would never dream of attending church, or of listening for a moment to an open-air service, will linger in the crowd at one of these meetings.

They are waiting for question-time, so that they may rend the speaker—metaphorically—limb from limb, or for some remark that will give an opening for a telling interjection.

The pulpit is sometimes called the "coward's castle"—because no one can reply to what is said in it.

But the parson who goes out—as does my friend Donald Soper to his weekly lunch-hour meetings at Tower Hill—to stand on a soap box, or an exposed bit of wall, or a portable platform, in competition with rival orators, whose subjects range from Communism to vivisection, from money reform to some personal grievance against authority, has to take on every opponent who offers himself.

Often his meetings will be rather like a dog-fight. Humorists will try to raise a laugh at his expense.

He may find himself up against merciless

heckling—be asked questions which he cannot answer.

Among those who haunt the meetings in the open-air forums of our great cities are some men of wide knowledge and considerable ability.

They may be scholars who are paying the price of folly—or worse than folly.

They may be working-men who have devoted the leisure of a lifetime to self-education. They may be the enthusiasts of some cause.

Perhaps they join the attack from an itch for disputation—or to prove to themselves that their tongue has not lost its cunning.

More frequently, they believe that religion is the opium of the people, and are eager to expose the "dope peddler."

Whatever their motives, they are formidable antagonists. A young parson need feel no humiliation in sometimes having to give them best.

But, you may ask, how is it possible to advance the cause of Christianity if you are bested in argument and made to look foolish? How can you hope to do any good that way?

I shall take an extreme case first—the case of a young man who, week after week, was pursued relentlessly by the same heckler, a militant "free-thinker" who was a really brilliant man.

The youngster had neither the knowledge nor the intellectual resources of his tormentor.

But he always drew a big crowd—people knew that the heckler would provide the fireworks.

So it went on for about two months.

Then one day, after a particularly devastating repartee had convulsed the crowd, the free-thinker exclaimed scornfully: "If I couldn't put up a better show than you do, I shouldn't come back."

"I wouldn't come back either," said the young man, "if I thought about it like that. You don't imagine I enjoy being laughed at, do you?

"But I'd rather be laughed at than stop preaching what I know to be the truth.

"And don't you think," he turned to the crowd, "that I must have hold of something worth while before I'm willing to be made the butt of someone so much cleverer than myself to bear witness to it?"

It was the perfect answer. It turned every one of the free-thinker's former triumphs into evidence against him.

But, as a general rule, an open-air religious meeting needn't be such an ordeal as this young man found it.

These clever antagonists of whom I have been speaking usually go for what they consider the weakest part of your case. They attack the Churches.

There is a great deal that may be said against the Churches as they are with some show of truth.

But if you are primarily concerned with Christianity, that needn't worry you.

Almost every charge that is made against the Churches is, when you come to analyse it, essentially this: that they have failed to live up to the teaching and example of Christ.

And even the bitterest enemies of organized religion pay tribute to Our Lord when, as they so frequently do, they appeal from some aspect of the Church to the carpenter of Nazareth.

These open-air meetings may thus serve a double purpose.

They bring the simple, central truths of Christianity before large numbers of people. And they inspire those who conduct them to try, to the utmost of their power, to bring their Churches nearer to the Christian ideal.

When, in my East London days, I used to speak in Victoria Park, and at other meetings of this kind where I have spoken since, I found that one of the biggest stumbling-blocks is the quarrels of sects and denominations.

Even if these open-air meetings did nothing else, they would be worth while if they could only convince Christians of the folly of petty jealousies and bickerings, and extended the area of that friendly co-operation which is already coming into being.

But they do much else. A number of the questions put are concerned with real difficulties, and often with difficulties which are felt by many besides the questioner.

If the right answer can be found, it may be a turning-point in a life.

It is, indeed, impossible to set a limit to what may be done in this way.

A few months ago I was on Tower Hill with Donald Soper.

What I saw convinced me, not only of the value of his work, but of the vast field which lies open and the magnificent results that might be obtained if only more of the right men would take up the challenge.

Here, indeed, is one hopeful way of bringing religion to the people. There are others.

But there are also certain dangers in attempts to "popularize" Christianity, which enthusiasts sometimes fall into. If I may, I will refer to such matters later.

THERE are people who think that the whole
duty of man can be summed up in a series of
"Don'ts."

Listening to them, we almost get the impression
that the best way to Heaven is to stand still and
do nothing. All the commandments they lay
upon us are negative ones.

That doesn't make the Heavenward path so very
much easier, however. There are so many things
that, according to them, we shouldn't do. And
they're always finding new ones to add to their
list.

"If anybody does it, it's wrong," seems to be
their slogan. They are like the mother who said
to her eldest daughter: "Go out and see what
Tommy is doing, and tell him not to."

Now there are lots of things we mustn't do.
But men and women, like children, get restive
if they have too many "don'ts" thrown at them.

That's one reason why it is unwise to multiply
prohibitions. If we do, people may end by paying
no attention to any of them. They'll ignore the
essential ones as well as those that are non-essen-
tial.

"I'm afraid I've had rather a wild life," a Scot

once said to me. "You see, I'm a minister's son."

When I told him I didn't quite see the connexion he laughed.

"There's a proverb in Scotland: 'The nearer the kirk, the further frae grace,'" he explained. "So many clergymen's sons kick over the traces as soon as they get away from home. They've been brought up so strictly that they go to the other extreme the moment they're free."

While we must have "Don'ts," therefore, it's best to cut them down to the minimum. And, wherever possible, we might turn them the other way round. For instance, instead of saying "Don't tell lies," we can say "Always tell the truth." Or we might substitute "Keep smiling" for "Don't pull a long face."

Often, indeed, we don't need to say anything. In dealing with children or young people the thing that really counts is example. They model their behaviour not on what we tell them, but on what we do.

I remember watching a handicraft instructor teaching a group of lads how to make things. He told them what he wanted them to do—and showed them how to do it.

Then they carried on while he passed from one boy to another, noting how they shaped.

Whenever the came to one who was doing the job wrongly, he stopped him. But he didn't say: "Don't do this" or "Don't do that." He said: "Do it like this"—and showed the lad the right

way all over again. Or he guided his hand as he
worked.

"Once learn to do a thing correctly," he said,
"and you'll get it right always."

Another thing he said was: "There are a
thousand wrong ways of doing anything, and only
one right one. I don't have time to warn you
against all the mistakes you might make—and
I don't need to. Learn the proper way thoroughly,
and it'll become second nature."

It's just the same with conduct. If our way of
life is right, we don't need eternally to be reminded
not to do certain things. We don't do them
because they don't fit in with the scheme of behaviour that has become instinctive.

That's not to say that we are perfect. None of
us is that. We still fall to our own particular
temptations.

But the grosser sins don't tempt us. We are
protected against them by right thinking, right
feeling, and right doing.

These things have become habitual. They are
part of our character.

A great many of the "Don'ts" that are flung at
young people are inspired by the belief that their
character is still unformed—that they can't be
trusted to do right instinctively. So they are
warned against certain things, not because they
are bad in themselves, but because they may lead
to evil.

The weakness of that is that the youngsters know

these things are really innocent enough. So to forbid them creates resentment and rebellion. And this mood may carry them over the border-line into actual wrong-doing.

I know, for instance, strange as it may sound to readers, that a great many Churchpeople are worried about dancing. They would like to keep young people away from dances because of the temptations they may encounter.

Or, while they might see no great harm in an occasional dance, they think that there are too many dances nowadays.

"You're always dancing," they say to eager-eyed girls, off for an evening's enjoyment. "You'd be far better to stay at home and read a good book."

There are even clergymen who preach against dancing, or write about its "dangers" in their parish magazines.

Now, there are dance-halls which are undesir-able places, frequented by undesirable people. But the decent youngster doesn't go to these places. Or, if he goes once, he doesn't go back.

And the young people whose character is still unformed—who may be led astray by bad com-pany?

We might shut up every dance-hall in the country and they'd still fall into bad company. And though we shout "Don'ts" at them till we're black in the face it won't make the slightest difference. They'll do what they want to do.

Well, let them do it. Let them dance. But let

us give them the chance to get their dancing in a healthy atmosphere, and with good, not bad, companions.

I believe that the Church should be a centre of social life. The building of Christian character is an essential part of its job.

But we can't build character by preaching at people on Sundays. They must build it for themselves in living.

And it is there—in their lives—that we must be in touch with them, and help them to do it.

Church dances, church social functions generally, church clubs for young people, can be a tremendous force for good. They can be made to build character, to teach the lesson of right living, in the best of all possible ways—by the power of example.

They represent the positive, as against the negative, approach. Instead of saying: "Don't go to dances," we say: "Come to our dances"—and make these as cheerful and attractive as we possibly can.

If we do that, we don't need to tell the young people that an undesirable dance-hall is wicked. They won't want to go there anyway—because they prefer the crowd that attend our dances and find them better fun.

Not only that, but we'll be in touch with the youngsters. We'll win their confidence. We'll get to know them, and they'll get to know us. We'll be able to help them to develop into the men and women of character that God meant them to be.

We can't help them so long as they write us down as "kill-joys."

And we can't be "kill-joys" without denying and betraying Our Lord—the Christ Who rejoiced with the wedding guests at Cana and loved to hear the laughter of children at their play.

PASSING a teashop belonging to a well-known firm of caterers, a wit remarked that once the Christians fed the lions, but now Lyons fed the Christians.

It is really remarkable how familiar we all are, from infancy, with the idea of lions and their prejudice against vegetarianism.

To the very young it brings a peculiar joy, tinged perhaps with just a shade of delicious fear to give an edge to excitement. Play lions with a three-year-old, and your popularity is assured.

There are many references to lions in Scripture —more, probably, than to any other wild animal. And we continue to encounter them in the records and legends of the Church.

Stories about them are recurring constantly in the lives of the saints and martyrs and—in modern times—of the missionaries.

The latest was published in the newspapers a week or so ago. It came from Rhodesia.

A missionary, it appeared, was walking through thick scrub to visit some of his converts when suddenly a lion jumped out from behind a bush.

This missionary was on foot, and the lion looked rather alarming as it lolloped towards him

Its intentions may have been amicable, but it seemed to him that the animal was in a temper.

What was he to do? He breathed a prayer and flung the Bible he was carrying straight at the lion. It dropped dead.

Recovering his Bible, the missionary returned thanks for his deliverance and resumed his journey. Rounding a corner, he found a man cleaning his rifle.

I have been surprised at the number of letters I have received asking me to comment on this incident.

"Isn't it rather a tall story?" inquire some of my correspondents. Others want to know if I think it was the prayer or the Bible that saved the missionary, or if the presence of the man with the gun was just coincidence.

It doesn't really matter how far every little detail of this story is correct. We needn't bother about that.

But what is interesting and important is the question it suggests to us: What is the place and function of prayer in our lives?

Prayer comes naturally to us in danger or emergency, or when we are in the shadow of illness or bereavement. At such times we turn to God as instinctively as a hurt or frightened child seeks the refuge of its mother's arms.

But are our prayers answered? Can they save us, for instance, from lions?

The Rhodesian missionary, very possibly,

thinks that they can. Sir John Gayre, Lord
Mayor of London nearly three hundred years ago,
was very sure of it when he provided in his will
for the annual Lion Sermon at the Church of
St. Katharine Cree, which I was invited to preach
last year.

Sir John had been shipwrecked. As he knelt in
prayer a lion approached him, sniffed all round,
and then made off.

In this case it may well be that prayer did save
the shipwrecked man. But while he himself might
have said that he was "protected" while he knelt,
it was probably the unfamiliar attitude, the still-
ness and calm of the man who was praying, that
first puzzled the lion, and then led him to look
elsewhere for a victim.

To say that is not to belittle the power of
prayer.

It was the sense of communion with God, that
he had placed himself in God's hands, that gave
Sir John Gayre the strength and courage to remain on his knees while the lion prowled round
him.

In a similar way, even without the man with the
gun, our Rhodesian missionary might have
escaped.

The fact that he faced up to the lion, the
unfamiliar missile thrown at it so boldly, might
have disconcerted the animal and made it turn
tail.

We *are* "protected" when we pray. We are

"protected" in the sense that we are given new faith, new confidence, new courage.

It is in a somewhat similar way that prayer may help us in illness. We pray for health, and sometimes—it seems almost as if by a miracle—health is restored to us.

There are many astonishing instances of this—examples of what is called faith healing. Belief in that is not superstition.

Prayer in cases of illness brings the patient into the frame of mind where he will receive the greatest benefit from the doctor's treatment, and in which the healing processes of nature are given their full value.

That, you may say, is something purely natural; we aren't entitled to say that it represents an answer to prayer. It *is* purely natural—but it is God Who is the Great Architect of Nature. This relation between mind and body is His handiwork.

And the strength and consolation that we derive from prayer do come from God. I believe that He does hear our prayers and does answer them—in His own way.

Wherever we go, whatever dangers we encounter, whatever suffering or sorrow we may know, we are in His hands.

While we have the sense of God's abiding presence and enduring love, nothing can harm us—death itself, however it may come, is only the last step upon the road that brings us in the end to Him.

IN the train the other day I overheard a remark made by a mother to her son, a boy of about fourteen.

The lad was reading, and chuckling as he read.

"I can't understand," said the mother, "what you see in that rubbish. There are plenty of good books you ought to read—and you waste your time on that!"

As the train roared on, I recalled a little story told by Mr. Cyril Asquith in the "Life of Lord Oxford and Asquith," which he wrote with Mr. J. A. Spender.

One day in 1925 Mrs. Cyril Asquith discovered the old statesman absorbed in a popular magazine—and asked what he was reading.

Asquith looked slightly embarrassed.

"As a matter of fact," he said, "it's a story called 'Archie and the Sausage-chappie.'" Then, more confidently, he added: "It's very good; it's by P. G. Wodehouse."

Later, his son learned that the ex-Premier had "unobtrusively consumed almost the entire output of this author."

I like that story. The grave political leader,

aloof and austere, as so many of us remember him, suddenly comes closer—is revealed in a new and very human light.

If a census could be taken of the reading of public men, it would probably afford other surprises.

Mr. Lloyd George, I believe, has a weakness for detective fiction. And there is a well-known Socialist M.P. who prefers Wild West stories to any other literature.

Can such reading be dismissed—as the woman in the train dismissed it—as "waste of time?"

Most of us suspect guiltily that it is a waste of time.

But we cannot all be like the late Dr. Temple, who, when Archbishop of Canterbury, used to take a volume of algebra upstairs with him to read in bed. We prefer lighter fare.

And why not? Even if we feel, in Cecil Rhodes' phrase, that there is "so little time, so much to do," we cannot go on working at high pressure indefinitely.

Our minds, as well as our bodies, demand relaxation and recreation. We are able to work all the better if we allow ourselves an occasional break.

It may only be half an hour with an amusing book or a crossword puzzle before we turn out the light and go to sleep.

But we shall sleep all the better because we have switched our mind off the problems and worries of the day.

There are times, too, when we are ill, or run down, or over-tired. Sleep eludes us, and we lie, tossing restlessly from side to side, through the long, heavy-footed hours. What a blessing it is to be able to turn to a favourite author, or to have a crossword to work out.

Personally, I must confess that crossword puzzles are beginning to fascinate me. I never see one without wanting to seize a pencil and start filling in the blanks.

I no longer feel guilty about it. I save the crosswords for a time when I am tired or wake up in the middle of the night and cannot sleep again.

And I feel very grateful to the man who invented them. He is a public benefactor.

Don't say, please, that this is all very well for invalids and those who suffer from insomnia—but that it is still a waste of time for other people.

There is a story of a great scientist who lamented, in his old age, that he could not read poetry.

He felt that he had missed a great deal because of that—but it was too late to remedy the deficiency. Poetry was utterly meaningless to him.

The power of poetical appreciation had withered away by disuse. He had killed it. And now—when he wished to do so—he could not bring it to life again.

It is like that with other things.

If we go on, year after year, never relaxing,

never "letting up," never "wasting our time," we will find, when illness comes, or work fails us, that we have no resources, that there is nothing to fill the empty hours.

We may have warning of this in advance. It's a danger signal if, on holiday, we keep wondering what is happening at the office or at the works, and feel bored and "fed-up" with our temporary idleness.

Sometimes it is said that a man's work is his life. But it isn't—or, at least, it ought not to be—the whole of his life.

There can be no true happiness without work, but a life that is all work is too one-sided. There should be laughter in life as well—and warmth and humanity.

Reading and solving crosswords are solitary pursuits. But they prepare us for human relationships and facilitate human contacts.

We see a man reading in a railway carriage, or on the deck chair beside ours, and notice that his book is by one of our favourite authors. Immediately we feel drawn towards him. When, presently, he puts down the book, conversation starts easily and naturally. A common enthusiasm paves the way. And so we are enriched by association with a new mind.

It doesn't matter that the association is purely temporary—a holiday acquaintanceship, or a matter of half an hour's talk. We have touched life at yet another point.

Or someone looks up from a crossword puzzle,

and says: "A word of six letters, meaning 'cut out,'" and we sit up and weigh in with suggestions.

Again the ice has been broken.

A common interest in "trifles"—if we must call them that—can be a bond, almost as much as a common interest in a cause.

And it has this value of its own, that it cuts across differences of outlook and helps us to recognize something akin to ourselves in those from whom we may differ violently.

When, a year or two ago, the late Sir Austen Chamberlain admitted to a liking for crosswords, a great many who shared this taste, but were opposed wholeheartedly to his politics, had a new revelation of the man.

And there have been times, in difficult and delicate negotiations between employers and trade unionists, when a pause for tea and sandwiches has enabled conversation to bring to light tastes and pursuits in common.

When the discussion has been resumed, there has been a new spirit in it—a readiness to see the other fellow's point of view and to meet him half-way.

The break for refreshments has been the turning point. Something relatively unimportant—having nothing to do with the matters at issue—has built a bridge between conflicting interests.

No. I don't think there is any need for us to be ashamed of our liking for detective stories, or humour, or crossword puzzles—or any similar pleasant and innocent way of "wasting time."

These things bring ease and forgetfulness in illness; they lighten sleepless hours; they add zest to leisure; and, on occasion, they help us to get to know and like our fellow men.

There is no need to apologize for anything that does that.

THE CUP FINAL AND "ABIDE WITH ME"

I DON'T know whether the great crowd at Wembley's next Cup Final will sing *Abide with me* while they are waiting for the Cup Final to begin.

It has been sung before on such occasions, and there have been protests about it. *Abide with me*, we are told, is not intended for community singing at gatherings of this kind.

Once, in France during the war, a colonel came up to me and exclaimed: "You must stop the men, padre. They're singing hymn-tunes and fitting their own words to them."

He was horrified. And certainly the words these soldiers were singing weren't pretty.

But they had been through hell. They were going back to hell.

They were singing the old familiar tunes for the comfort they got from them.

And they supplied their own words because they didn't like to admit they needed that comfort.

I tell that story to bring home the wonderful power of some of those old hymns.

It's not only the words or the music which gives that power.

It's their associations.

Abide with me is one of the most beautiful of them all.

It is also, for many of us, pregnant with the most intimate and sacred memories.

I don't think it is possible to sing it without emotion. The effect of a great concourse singing it is moving in the extreme.

But on an occasion like a Cup Final, what should be a great spiritual experience becomes merely a sort of emotional cocktail.

Abide with me is forgotten in the thrills of an athletic contest.

All the passions of partisanship are unleashed close on the heels of a beauty that has lit the darkness of many a death-bed and brought healing to the generations of them that mourn.

I am no kill-joy. I would prefer to see more people playing games themselves and fewer merely watching.

I know, however, that for great numbers the Saturday football match is the only real recreation of the week.

They have every right to enjoy it.

But don't let us lose our sense of proportion.

We would object to *Abide with me* being sung as a curtain-raiser to a revue.

It is just as much out of place on the football ground.

That's not to say religion has nothing to do with sport.

If a man's religion is real it will affect the way he plays, or watches, games, just as it affects everything else he does.

Man is a whole.

What a man is in himself, the pattern of his life, shows in his every activity. He doesn't stop being himself because he's "up for the Cup."

If he's a true Christian he'll be a true sportsman.

He won't condone dirty play or unfair tactics because they gain a goal for the side he wants to win.

But he won't need to sing *Abide with me* before the game to remind himself he is that sort of man.

And the other "win-at-any-price" man will sing the hymn with the rest.

Then, in half an hour or less, he'll want to kill the referee because of a decision against the side he backed in his pool coupon.

Yet, just because he's sung *Abide with me* and got a cheap emotional thrill out of it, on top of all the thrills of the match, he'll think he's something of a fellow and as good a Christian as those people who go to church.

Perhaps he is—but he isn't as good a Christian as those who try to live Christ-like lives. They, indeed, are the only Christians there are.

It's the old story of the "muscular" Christianity so popular in Victorian days.

Then there were far too many who seized on the phrase, but interpreted it, in practice, as all muscle and no Christianity.

It won't do.

Let us enjoy our football and other healthy sports.

Let us live our religion in our recreation as in our work and our homes. But don't let us cheapen sacred things merely to get an additional "kick" into an exciting Saturday afternoon at Wembley.

Actually a sense of what is fitting should suggest to us, I venture to submit, that there are times when it is not desirable to sing *Abide with me*, which hymn ends with the words:—

> Hold Thou Thy cross before my closing eyes,
> Shine through the gloom, and point me to the skies;
> Heaven's morning breaks and earth's vain shadows flee;
> In life, in death, O Lord, abide with me.

Those who desire to use words like these at Wembley are guilty not of blasphemy, but of bad taste—at least, that is my opinion.

"I DON'T understand my children at all. Their minds are a closed book to me. They keep me at arm's length. We might as well be strangers!"

How often do we hear a father say this? And have you noticed that it is always a father who says it? It is never a mother.

The bond between mother and child is, of course, the closest in nature. Mother-love is the deepest, most elemental, most permanent emotion of all.

And the child, though it out-grows its early dependence, still turns instinctively to its mother in times of difficulty and distress.

But that does not explain why so many children are "strangers" to their fathers. The strength of the one bond does not account for the weakness of the other.

What does explain it, I think, is the fact that many fathers see far too little of their children, and take no trouble to understand what they do see. They seldom enter into a child's life as the mother does; they remain permanently on the outside.

As they conceive it their duty to a child is

finished when they provide for its material needs. All the rest is the mother's job.

It isn't exactly fair to the mother to ask her to shoulder the whole of this great responsibility. Nor is it much use to say, as I have heard some fathers say:—

"I'll see to the youngsters when they're a bit older. It's then that a father counts."

If the foundations of trust and confidence between father and child aren't laid in early childhood it is very difficult to establish them later on. It's the early years that matter.

Of course, in the early years the father is handicapped. Five days a week the only time he sees the children is in the mornings, when he is rushing to get to work. When he returns home they are asleep.

Week-ends should put the balance right. But they don't always do so. A football match or a game of golf or a bicycle run may seem a better way of spending a Saturday afternoon than taking the children out.

I recall the story of the little girl who was asked in class what she knew about Sunday. She replied: "It's the day father stays in bed, and I mustn't make a noise."

Even when father doesn't stay in bed sometimes he "can't be bothered with the kids." Sunday is the only free day he has.

He never stops to think that his wife hasn't a free day at all, and that she probably needs rest and change at least as much as he does.

8

The tragedy of it is that, in such circumstances, both father and child are missing something that cannot be replaced or made good.

Every child needs the love and care of both parents—if too much is left to the mother, there is danger of lop-sided development.

And the father's neglect is not only creating a gulf that nothing can bridge in the years to come —it is also depriving him, now, of a very satisfying and delightful companionship.

For it is a profound mistake to think that there can be no true companionship between a child and a man. We cannot, indeed, give a child a man's thoughts or a man's knowledge. Nor is that desirable.

But the child can lead us into the kingdom of youth, which is the nearest thing to the Kingdom of Heaven earth can offer.

So I would say to every father who has been "leaving the youngsters to the wife":

Get to know your children.

Take them off their mother's hands for a few hours when you can.

Try to enter sympathetically into their lives and thoughts.

Holiday time is a good opportunity. You can get close to your children, and they can get close to you, building sand castles or inspecting the rock pools.

But—don't try to "boss" them. And don't help them too much. Let them do it for themselves.

Even if you think they can't manage a thing, so long as it isn't dangerous, let them try. They'll ask for assistance if they find they need it.

Above all, don't force a child to bathe, or even to wade, in the sea. The sea can be terrifying to a small child.

I remember witnessing the first introduction of a two-year-old to the ocean.

"That," said the father, "is the sea."

"Too big a bath," said his son, and turned his back on it.

To move too quickly in such a case may give a child a permanent distaste for salt water. It may also destroy the confidence that is growing up between you.

Let him go in in his own time—or, if he so decides, not at all.

You will learn a great deal about your child by listening intelligently to what he says.

A child knows when you are not really attending to him—and resents it. And you can do a lot of harm by saying "naughty" too quickly.

For instance, a young child uses sound experimentally. He makes up sound combinations and tries them out. Sometimes, in so doing, he hits on a "swear word." Remember, it isn't swearing to him.

He doesn't know what swearing is.

Or, perhaps a little later, he seizes eagerly on every new word he hears. Occasionally, perhaps, he hears a word that is unfortunate. He adopts that too.

Should you, in either case, make a fuss about it, all you succeed in doing nine times out of ten is to fix the word in his memory. If you ignore it, the chances are that he will forget all about it.

Even the vicar's children probably had one or two curious words in their vocabulary when they were round about the same age.

Then I remember a father coming to me in great distress of mind. His son, he had discovered, was a liar. I asked how old the boy was and what sort of lies he had been telling.

The young man, it appeared, was five. He had not only assured his father that "Wee Willie Winkie" had come to see him while he was in bed—he had stuck to the story in spite of all remonstrances.

Your child may tell you similar stories.

He may repeat conversations he has had with the dog, or with the cat at home, or with his toy animals.

He will relate, quite seriously, the most impossible tales.

But don't call him a liar. He isn't telling lies.

During the early years of a child's life, he lives very largely in a world of imagination and make-believe. That world is real to him—and it merges into his everyday surroundings, or they merge into it.

To really get to know a child, you must be prepared to enter into these imaginings. You must learn to look at the world through his eyes and see familiar things with the sunrise glow of wonder upon them.

Finally, don't stand on your dignity, or cherish inflated ideas about what your children "owe" to you.

If, in helping a youngster to sail a boat, you do something he does not like, he won't mince his words in telling you about it. And at times he may give you still ruder shocks.

"I don't like you, Daddy," a four-year-old boy remarked to a friend of mine recently.

"What did you say?" I asked him.

"What could I say?" he replied. "I felt a bit hurt—and then I suddenly realized what it really meant.

"When I was a small boy I shouldn't have dared to say anything like that to my father. There would have been an awful hullabaloo. I should have been told I was wicked and probably sent supperless to bed. But my son wasn't in the least afraid to say it to me.

"He knew that he could say just what was in his mind at the moment—that he could be perfectly frank, that there was no need to pretend. That seems a pretty good basis to build on."

It is a good basis to build on. And you will have every cause for congratulation if, at the end of your holiday, your children are on similar terms of frankness and trust with you.

D<small>O</small> you know the schoolboy's translation of *"L'Anglais avec son sangfroid habituel?"*

It is: "The Englishman with his usual bloody cold."

Influenza is now in season. I know all about it. I've just had it myself.

Why shouldn't I claim the privilege of convalescents and talk about my illness?

'Flu is a subject of universal interest. Most of us have had it, and who knows whether we shan't have it again?

Of course, you may dodge it this winter. Here's hoping you will.

But suppose you don't—what are you going to do with it?

And suppose you only get a cold that keeps you in a day or two, and you are lucky enough to be able to stay at home, what are you going to do about that? Are you going to use it?

At first blush, I suppose, the idea of using an illness sounds silly. How is it possible? Surely illness is just something to endure with as much patience as we can summon to our aid.

That isn't quite true. Illness is like everything else. It is an experience and an opportunity

(I've had my whack, and I really know this time of what I speak).

We can ignore an opportunity, we can misuse it, or we can turn it to account. We can extract from every experience whatever of good or ill it has to offer us.

Influenza is an infernal nuisance, but provided it doesn't cost us our job it needn't be a calamity.

It may even be a benevolent trick of nature to compel us to take the rest that mind and body are needing so badly.

That is one reason why it is so foolish to try to go on working when the 'flu is on you.

There are other reasons, of course, including the risk of infecting others. Though I believe we may get good out of 'flu I don't believe in broadcasting its benefits.

When you go to bed don't fuss and start taking your temperature and feeling your pulse every hour.

If we are to make anything of 'flu or any other illness we must learn to treat it philosophically; to relax and not to worry.

It may help quite a bit to use an enforced idleness to do some of the things we haven't had time for when we were well. Those books we wanted to read, for instance, but weren't able to tackle while we were working at full pressure—now's our chance!

I have a friend who declares that he relies on his annual bout of 'flu to get abreast of his reading. "I don't know how I'd manage without it," he once told me.

Here may I be allowed a word of caution? Many modern books are hardly suitable for depressed minds.

Read a "thriller" now and then if you like, but don't specialize on the stuff that makes you want to bite the bedclothes when you do drop off to sleep.

I find it a good plan to mix my reading when I'm ill.

I like to have quite a few books handy—books that have been read and re-read, as well as a few new ones.

The theory is that I dip into them all. Sometimes I do. But more often I find myself so caught up in the spell of a familiar magic that I read solidly through, say, a Jane Austen or one of the novels of Charles Dickens before I ever glance at any of the newer volumes.

How often now one meets young people who don't seem to know the old writers. If they tackled *Bleak House* or *David Copperfield* or George Borrow's *Lavengro* the next time they had an attack of influenza they might vote the illness a blessing in disguise.

It is lovely, too, at times to read good strong poetry and then to lie and think about it and allow it to get to work inside you. And there's a lot to be said even for learning a fresh game when we are ill—chess or draughts, for instance.

That brings me to another of the ways—I believe the most important way—in which influenza or any other illness may be useful to us. It gives us time to think.

It is the curse of modern life that we are always in a hurry—that we are very rarely able just to sit down and take thought.

In illness, the flying minutes slow to a walking pace. There are hours when time seems almost to stand still. We may get horribly bored because of that—but we needn't. We can ask ourselves some of those big questions we keep putting on one side while we are rushing from one job of work to another.

Some of these questions, indeed, will probably rise unbidden. There are very many people who never think about God and religion except when they are ill. But they do think of them then.

It is no use saying that this is merely because they have the wind up. In most cases fear has little to do with it.

The truth is that our day-to-day activities are, very often, a screen shutting us off from God. When we are ill, that screen is often thrown down.

The very weakness of our body may bring Him nearer to us—perhaps because we need Him more; and because the walls of flesh that imprison the spirit have grown thin, almost transparent, like gossamer that even a breath may blow aside. It is as though the rhythm of the body must be slowed down before the rhythm of the spirit can assert itself.

The lives of saints and mystics give us many

examples of spiritual strength growing out of physical frailty.

I am not suggesting that it is only when we are ill that we can be in communion with God. But it is easier to establish communication, to come to a knowledge of God and of what He means for us, when the spiritual faculties have been sharpened and made stronger in relation to our bodies.

That happens in illness, as it happens in the hour of bereavement, or when we are overwhelmed with anxiety for some loved one.

It is well to take advantage of it. If, when we are on a sick-bed, religion becomes real to us and we are made aware of the reality of God, we shall carry something from that experience back into daily life when we recover.

ONCE, in the days before hiking became popular, I met a middle-aged man on a lonely moorland road. We talked and he told me of long walks which he had taken.

"You must be very fond of walking," I said.

"Oh, I don't know," he replied. "But if I stay at home the women go jabber, jabber, jabber. And this is the only way I can get away from them."

Well, he wouldn't be able to escape so easily now. The women of to-day will walk mile for mile with the men.

Often, indeed, they are more energetic and swing along quite cheerfully while "the stronger sex" lags behind and wonders whether it wouldn't be better to catch the bus at the next village.

But that man of the old days is significant. He helps us to realize how remarkable—and how healthy—a change has occurred during recent years.

Never before have so many people walked for pleasure. To our grandfathers walking wasn't a pleasure. It was a means of getting somewhere, or, as in the case of the man on the moorland road, of getting away from something.

No doubt, then as now, there were people who loved the beauty of the countryside, who knew every field and footpath, every turn of the winding lanes, every coppice and cottage, every laughing brook and shadowed pool for miles around.

But they were usually people who didn't have to work for their living—or didn't work too hard for it.

Often, too, their love of the country was a by-product of the management of a farm or an estate or of some favourite sport.

And these people didn't live in the towns and work in factories or shops or offices.

Those who did that were too tired, when Sundays or holidays came round, for active exercise.

They didn't want to go into the country, any-way—they preferred the bar parlour to the hill-side; the jostling crowd in fair-ground or market-place and the shouts of the cheapjacks to the wind on the heath.

Even to the great majority of those who were born among them, the country sights and sounds and smells meant little or nothing in terms of beauty or enjoyment.

The villagers worked too hard; often they hadn't enough to eat. The loveliest scenery on earth doesn't make much appeal to the under-nourished.

You need a full stomach as well as a seeing eye to appreciate the pageant of Nature. To a hungry man a steak will always look better than a sunset.

Yet, somehow, those who left the countryside

for the towns or for far lands overseas could never forget this background of youth and early manhood.

All their lives thereafter they were homesick for the fields and woods to which they had paid so little conscious heed.

Even then, of course, they didn't care about the country as country. It was just one particular place to which they wanted to return.

And they didn't think of it as being beautiful. For the most part beauty didn't exist in their scheme of things. They thought of it as home.

Their children didn't share their feeling. They couldn't understand it. To them the mean streets were home—or the rolling Canadian prairies, or the Australian bush.

But to-day the people of the towns—the descendants of those exiles from the rural scene of long ago—have rediscovered the country.

In an age when sophisticated pleasures are more numerous—and cheaper—than in any past period, they have learned the deep joy of simple things. And they care for the country as country—care for it consciously.

They have a real appreciation of its beauty.

Also they have found that exercise is fun—that there is real satisfaction in doing things and going to places under your own power.

So, even while mechanical transport has been brought to an unheard-of perfection and road services have been extended to embrace all but the remotest villages, more and more young people have decided that legs are made to walk with.

What all that means in fullness of life is incalculable. And it will mean more and more as the years go by.

So let us welcome hiking—this urge that, every week-end and Bank Holiday, sends the youth of Britain striding out, rucksack on back, "over the hills and far away."

I know there are some clergymen who shake their heads over it.

They say that young people are spending their Sundays in the country when they ought to be attending church.

Personally, I don't worry too much about that. Many of these hikers are going where very few of them will be, for the whole of Sunday, out of earshot of the bells that call to prayer.

They may not think that call is addressed to them.

But here and there parsons in charge of country churches are saying to the ramblers: "Come and join us in our service. Never mind if you're wearing only shirts and shorts. You are entirely welcome." And the hikers come.

If more parsons took this line, set out actively to attract these young people to their churches—or, as some others have done, organized special open-air services at favourite beauty spots—this rediscovery of the country might well be the prelude to a rediscovery of religion.

But even without such efforts on the part of the Church, hiking should help, rather than hinder, the cause of religion.

It is easy to forget God in a town. It is not so easy when the hush of twilight falls upon the world and one by one the stars come out overhead.

Oh, I know that we can see the stars in town as well. But usually we don't. We don't look up.

I believe that the path across the moors and over the hills that the hikers are taking is a path that may lead in the end to God.

DID you know that hiking was wicked?
I didn't know it either—until a few letters rolled in telling me all about it.

Apparently I had overlooked what one of my correspondents calls "the grave moral dangers of mixed walking."

It's a bit of a mouthful, isn't it? But let's see what real substance there is behind the sounding phrase.

There are moral dangers in hiking—just as there are in everything else.

But we don't refuse to talk lest we should be tempted to lie, or to eat because we are afraid of the sin of gluttony.

Moral, like physical, danger is with us always. We can't dodge it. We must learn how to deal with it.

And the way to deal with it isn't to run away and hide. You know the story of the woman who took to her bed because, with all these accidents happening everywhere, it seemed the safest place.

"Stay in bed if you like," said her husband. "But remember, more people die in bed than anywhere else."

I'll admit right away that, when young men

and girls go hiking together, they may find opportunities for immorality. But these won't tempt any one who doesn't want to be tempted. So far as there is moral danger in hiking, it comes from ourselves.

The letters I received on this subject were from people who are still living in the Victorian age. I don't take them seriously.

But among them were two which do demand careful attention. They came from parents worried about sons or daughters who have taken up hiking or who wish to do so.

Don't think I fail to appreciate their anxiety.

But if their youngsters are the right sort, if they have been properly taught and trained, hiking can do them no harm. And if parents can't trust their children on a country ramble, then they can't trust them anywhere.

The other day, in a case at a juvenile court, a magistrate said: "A girl of sixteen has a right to rule her own life."

It's rather a sweeping statement—and I'm not prepared to endorse it fully. But there are girls of sixteen with jobs away from home who have to rule their own lives and who do it very creditably.

I would also say this: Every girl of sixteen should be learning how to rule her own life—and you can't train yourself to the proper use of freedom unless you have a certain amount of it.

To try to keep a girl from temptation by shutting her up is sheer folly. And if she is in danger of

9

"going wrong" she doesn't need to go hiking to find opportunities. She will get them in other ways.

She did get them in other ways long before hiking became a national habit.

As a matter of fact, hiking—real hiking, not the sham sort that is only an excuse for philandering—may be the means of saving her.

For hikers are a decent lot. You have only to talk to them to realize that.

The vast majority of them come from homes where marriage is still a partnership "for keeps." Such homes teach self-respect—and respect for others.

Some of my correspondents talked about the "weakness" of human nature.

I prefer to trust to the strength of human nature. Part of that strength lies in the fact that every one of us does instinctively respond to the good in others.

Put the sort of girl we're considering—the girl who might be corrupted by evil companions, because she has no fixed principles or real force of character—in a band of decent young people, and she'll be decent too.

She'll take her cue from them. And gradually, if the association continues, she will acquire the things she lacks.

By all means, if you're a parent, find out what sort of young people your girl—or your boy— wants to go hiking with. Encourage your youngsters to bring their friends home. You'll be able to tell if they're the right sort.

If you're doubtful, the way to deal with the situation isn't to forbid hiking to your sons and daughters. Encourage them, instead, to take it up seriously.

Get them to join a properly run rambling club. Tell them about the Youth Hostels Association and suggest they join it and take advantage of its facilities.

They'll learn then what hiking is and get in touch with the real hikers. And you needn't worry about them any more.

Vigorous outdoor exercise is in itself a way of keeping moral, as well as physical, health.

"There's nuthin' like work to take the devil out o' 'ee," an old countryman once said to me.

And a vigorous day's walking, if it isn't exactly work, still leaves the body healthily tired. It "takes the devil out of 'ee."

I cannot help thinking, too, that many of the fears expressed regarding hiking arise from a tendency to over-estimate the importance of sex to the young.

Our first love affairs are, as a rule, almost entirely sexless. There is much of reverence in them, and little of desire.

Think back to your own youth. Think of your shyness, your diffidence when you fell in love. Think how you idealized the loved one.

There is in life nothing that is more beautiful— or more pure—than this first blossoming. And the idyll gains an added sweetness if its scene is set in pleasant country lanes and amid meadow and woodland.

If country rambles lead to a boy-and-girl love affair, it will, usually, be to such an one as this. And interference—however well-meaning—may do infinite harm.

One final word to the doubters. We cannot guard our young people. They must find their own way, fight their own fight, deal with their own temptations.

What we can do—and what it is our duty to do—is to equip them for the pilgrimage of life. They are in our care in the formative years when character is built. If they fail us later on, it is because we have failed them then.

And it is useless to try to blame hiking, or anything else, for the results of our own short-comings.

IN days before we started talking learnedly of depressions over Iceland and high-pressure and low-pressure areas there was a Scottish minister who prayed for rain.

Before his petition there had been some weeks of abnormally dry weather. But during the six days that followed it did rain.

It rained too much—and too fiercely. The local farmers liked it no better than they had liked the dry spell.

When Sunday came again rain was still pouring down from a leaden sky. And the minister started his first prayer like this:—

"O Lord! we asked Thee for rain and Thou has sent it. We thank Thee, O Lord, but—dinna overdo it."

Holidaymakers are ready enough to make the best of things, but many of them must have thought that, this summer, the rain was overdoing it. True, the last week or so things have been better—but for large numbers of people the holidays have been spoiled.

Seaside landladies, too, have had a bad time.

Indeed, they are more to be pitied than their visitors. For the rest of us a wet summer is unpleasant. But there are thousands of landladies, struggling to make ends meet, to whom it threatens disaster.

I only hope they will be able to weather the storm.

But I am writing particularly for those who have been on holiday, or whose holiday is now drawing to a close.

Even when the weather has been kind and we have enjoyed ourselves, many of us are not really sorry to return home.

Holidays are a pleasant interlude, but our real life is at home. The old familiar household things have a welcoming look. It is good to see them again.

Perhaps it is mostly older people who think like this. Youth regards holidays rather differently.

They are more important—and more real and romantic—than the workaday world. For youth lives largely in its dreams, and on holiday sometimes dreams come true.

So youth works hard for the rest of the year and hopes for another good holiday twelve months later.

Seniors have a holiday to enable them to go on working.

But young people would get just as bored as their elders with a holiday that lasted too long. "All play and no work" makes Jack bored and miserable just as surely as "all work and no play" makes him dull.

A good many parents discover that in the holidays—when their children are at home with nothing to do and all day to do it in.

Work is something more than a necessary nuisance. It is a means of saving your soul alive. Herein lies the tragedy of the unemployed.

I encounter many weary souls. They belong mainly to people who don't know how to spend their hours of enforced leisure.

There has been an enormous increase in recent years in the number of women in better-class homes who suffer from "nerves."

It is sometimes due to the refusal of mother-hood, but more often to the way in which the small, easy-to-run flat, equipped with every labour-saving device, has replaced the house and garden of other days.

For the moment I'm not concerned with *why* women don't want babies, or why they prefer flats. They may have very good reasons. But they are left with a great deal of spare time on their hands. And they find, in all too many cases, that they have escaped from drudgery only to fall into the worse bondage of boredom.

You can be tired but happy. But you can't be both bored and happy at the same time.

I remember a man telling me, after a holiday, that he was "back to the curse of Adam."

He was thinking of the words "In the sweat of thy face shalt thou eat bread."

Call it a curse if you like. I don't think that it

is. There are places on earth where, such is the spontaneous bounty of nature, work is reduced to a minimum.

But it is from those lands where man has had to wrest his livelihood from a reluctant soil that the flower of civilization has sprung.

What has been true of the race is equally true of the individual.

So when we come home from the holidays and return to the daily round we aren't, as young people sometimes imagine, turning our backs on life. Work is life.

I am not forgetting, when I say that, the large number of people who are engaged in unsuitable or uncongenial labour. But they don't want to escape from work altogether. They want the sort of job they can enjoy doing.

There, probably, we have the answer to what, in these days, of a vastly increased industrial efficiency, is called the problem of leisure.

Too many holidays would make us just as uncomfortable as too many and too heavy meals. And, to alter slightly a famous epigram, if there were no work it would be necessary to invent it.

HOLIDAYS WITH PAY

A GREAT many of us take holidays far too much for granted. We are accustomed to going away every summer to seaside or country.

We spend a fair amount of money. And sometimes we have very little to show for it—except, perhaps, the after-effects of sunburn—when it is all over.

We try to cram so many activities and excitements into one short fortnight that we get "indigestion." So we come back feeling sick and sorry—and looking it.

Well, perhaps that does apply to the young people rather than to those of us who have reached years of discretion and know the bliss of a deck chair in the shade.

But, whether we spend our holidays wisely or misuse them, we'd feel cheated if we didn't get a summer vacation.

And we'd consider it disgraceful if we didn't receive our wages or salaries while we were away, if any one said to us: "No work, no money."

That, however, is just what their employers say to millions of our fellow countrymen and countrywomen. Those who don't have paid holidays are far more numerous than those who do.

And usually it is those who most need the break in routine who are denied it.

There are, I believe, about 11,500,000 insured workers in this country. Of these about 1,500,000 get holidays with pay.

The ten millions who don't include large numbers of low-wage workers who can't possibly afford to go away for a decent holiday if there's no money coming in.

If there are a few days without work, it's hard enough to scrape along at home.

At the other end of the scale there are those whose earnings take them out of the insured class altogether.

As a rule, the higher their salaries are, the longer are their holidays. And their pay goes on all the time.

It's true enough that the man who bears a burden of responsibility requires a really good vacation. And it's right and proper that he should get it.

But I can't believe that workers engaged, week after week, and month after month, on monotonous tasks, or whose jobs involve physical exertion, don't need a holiday too.

Many of them work in conditions that are unpleasant, if not actually unhealthy.

They live, crowded together, in mean streets. There is little comfort in their homes, little beauty in their lives, little joy in their work.

I know, of course, that the home atmosphere doesn't depend on money. It is astonishing, almost incredible, how bright and cheerful some women can make the most unpromising dwelling.

But there are thousands of people who, after all our slum clearances and housing schemes, are condemned to live in hovels that no amount of labour or ingenuity can redeem.

Even where the home-maker's efforts are successful, it is often at a terrific cost. The unending struggle to have things nice for husband and children takes toll of looks and health.

Still more than their menfolk, these women need rest and change—a break in the soul-destroying routine.

But what chance have they of getting it? If there is no holiday for their husbands, there is no holiday for them.

It is true that innumerable families do manage, by scraping and pinching for the rest of the year, to get a few days, or a week, at the seaside. But there are many who find it impossible.

I sometimes wonder if we realize just how many.

There are various children's holiday funds that take youngsters, whose lives would otherwise be bounded by city streets, into the country or to the sea for a day, or a week, or sometimes a fortnight.

But these funds are unable to cope with the need.

There are still too many children who have

never run on grass, or gathered wild flowers in the woods, or made sand castles, or bathed and paddled in the sea.

And even if we could give holidays to all these children, it would still leave untouched the parents' need.

We are beginning to realize that. There are holiday camps for unemployed workers in the distressed areas and elsewhere. A start has also been made with holidays for the wives of unemployed men.

These schemes are excellent. But, again, they only meet part of the need.

And they still leave untouched the problem of those who, though they are in jobs, don't earn enough to provide a decent holiday when every day without work is also a day without wages.

So I am particularly interested in the inquiry now being made into the general question of holidays with pay.

Doubts are expressed in many quarters as to whether it is an economic proposition.

Frankly, these doubts aren't impressive. One cannot help remembering the prophecies of doom that were made when child slavery in mines and factories was swept away.

Almost every reduction in hours or improvement in working conditions has been opposed as "impracticable" or "ruinous."

But our industries still survive. Wealth still accumulates.

Industry adapts itself to new conditions. And often it has been found that changes beneficial to the workers have also benefited their employers. It may be the same in this case.

For one thing, large sums are lost in industry every year because of illness. Some, at least, of this illness might well be prevented if every worker had an annual holiday of a week or a fortnight.

There is another argument that appears to be conclusive :—

In some twenty countries all wage-earners are entitled to holidays with pay; in a number of others this right is secured to large groups of workers by means of legislation.

None of them has come to disaster.

Are we going to lag behind?

It seems to me that those of us who enjoy adequate holidays, and who suffer no loss of income as a result of taking them, have a duty to those less fortunate than ourselves.

If we, who, for the most part, live in pleasant surroundings and have interesting work to do, need an annual break, how much more is a holiday necessary to those who don't share our advantages?

I think particularly of the children, who lose so much in health and happiness, and of the mothers, who put up so brave a fight against poverty.

I think of the men and women whose labours, in

many different spheres, contribute so much to our own comfort and well-being, whether at home or on holiday.

Surely common decency demands that we should put what voice and influence we possess behind the claim now made on their behalf—a claim which has been conceded in so many other countries.

I believe that wealth, whether national or individual, is a trust—and that Christianity provides the broad principles on which the trust should be administered.

And it seems absolutely incompatible with the Christian spirit that we should continue to deny this small measure of justice and relief to those to whose patient labours we owe so much.

Here, as I see it, is no question of politics. We are faced with a human need.

We have a moral obligation, a Christian duty, to see that it is met.

A NUMBER of people wrote to me a little time ago, pointing out that, as one of them puts it, "the Archbishop of York has put his foot down on this nonsense of 'Christian Pacifism,' and the Church Assembly has confirmed his view."

"I suppose," says another, "that, as a good democrat, you will now bow to the decision of the majority and stop preaching Pacifism."

Well, I hope that I'm a good democrat. But the value of democracy doesn't lie in the widsom of majority decisions. Majorities may be, and very often are, hopelessly in the wrong.

Democracy, by permitting even unpopular opinions to be expressed freely, helps to ensure that they don't stay permanently in the wrong. Its value is that it allows the free play of argument and criticism which, in the long run, should enable error to be rejected and truth to be established.

So—if a Pacifist may be allowed a military metaphor—I stick to my guns. And so do those who think with me.

The number of Christian Pacifists is not so inconsiderable as some of my correspondents suggest and as the voting in the Church Assembly might, indeed, lead them to believe.

Early this year more than seventy clergymen of the Church of England attended a private meeting at my house. They all believe that Christianity and war are incompatible.

None of them is going to climb down because of the Church Assembly. They have decided— in my opinion rightly—to carry on with the job of trying to convert the Church to Pacifism.

I don't intend to go into the general question here. But I think my correspondents are entitled to an answer as to why I cannot accept the Archbishop of York's statement and the vote of the Church Assembly as final and binding.

"It might," said Dr. Temple, "be my duty, in pursuing what is of higher value than life, to take life as well as to give my own. It can be a Christian duty to kill."

It may be a citizen's duty to kill—though there are those who think that killing is pretty futile, and men like Arthur Ponsonby, Aldous Huxley and Bertrand Russell, who look on the matter purely from the citizen's point of view, are reasonable people, not swayed by sentiment or vague idealism.

But, whether it is the duty of the citizen or not, I would maintain that it is not the duty of the Christian.

The archbishop says that it may be. He is a wiser man than I am, a more profound scholar. But if he is correct, then I have entirely misread my New Testament and misunderstood Christianity.

Dr. Temple, however, would probably define Christianity in much the same way as I would.

But he makes a distinction between the world as it is and the world as it ought to be. Only when the reign of law has been established, he says, will it be possible to go forward to the still higher claims of the Gospel.

I can see the force of this argument from the point of view of the citizen. But I think it is a tragedy that it should be put forward as the considered opinion of a leader of the Church.

It is no part of the function of the Church to adjust the Christian code to the practice of the world. It is the Church's job to make the world better, not to accept it as it is.

Christianity stands for a certain way of life. Those who profess it are not absolved from following that way of life because other people are content with less rigorous standards.

The fact that the rest of the world is in darkness is a strange reason for putting out the one light that remains.

Carried to its logical conclusion, the archbishop's argument would deny any real moral leadership to the Church. And I am convinced that it is only in so far as it is prepared to lead— to show the world the way of Christ—that the Church has any reason for existence.

I believe that the spirit of Christ can save the world.

I believe that it can reconcile the nations.

I believe that it can solve the problems which threaten to plunge us into war.

Why, then, ask us to forget it until a more convenient season—until the world has been saved, and the nations reconciled, and the problems solved without it?

Nothing of all this can be done without it.

What will happen, if Dr. Temple's view is universally accepted, is that the Church will become a sounding-board for the State, or for the League of Nations, and will cease to bear witness to those eternal principles of which it is the guardian and trustee.

That will be a disaster, not only for the Church, but for the world. It was very largely because, during the last war, the Churches in all the belligerent Powers were national rather than Christian that the peace, when it came, was vindictive.

I'm not talking to-day about the futility of war, or about the problem that an outbreak of hostilities may present to individuals called upon to decide between what they consider their duty as citizens and their duty as Christians, though I think that thoughtful citizens might come to realize that war wasn't an effective way of defending our property or of settling international disputes.

But as one who would like to be a decent follower of Jesus Christ I am persuaded that, whatever the consequences, this killing business is not to be done by a Christian.

If I did fall in with the majority, as I'm told I ought to, I should never see a German or an Italian without having at the back of my mind the thought: One day I may have to kill you.

I, for one, flatly refuse to put that into my attitude towards my neighbour. It seems to me the very negation of Christianity, and not all the casuistry of all the ecclesiastics of all the Churches will ever persuade me to the contrary.

THERE is a story, which some of you may have heard, of a vicar who called at the village school to ask a few simple questions about the Bible.

"Who led the children of Israel into Canaan?" he demanded.

The class looked at him blankly.

"Come now," he said, a little sharply, "who led the children of Israel into Canaan?"

A frightened voice answered from the front row: "Please, sir, it wasn't me. We only moved here last week."

That boy had an alibi. But there are times when we haven't an alibi—when, in fact, we can't have one. We've done something of which we feel heartily ashamed.

But even while we own up, or while we fight the matter out with our own conscience, the cry rises to our lips: "It wasn't I who did it!"

We're not attempting to deny the fact. We're not trying to plead "Not guilty." We're not placing the blame on any one else. We are trying to convince ourselves that this act of ours was a momentary aberration—something that is foreign to our character.

We did do this thing, whatever it was. But

we don't know why we did it. Looking back, we
can't understand it at all. It seems to us to have
been the act of another person.

Each of us, you see, has his own mental picture
of himself. It is usually a little kinder to his self-
esteem than the reality.

And it is rather a jolt when something happens
that falsifies the flattering portrait, makes us
question its truthfulness.

We want to forget the jarring note as quickly
as possible, to get back to our former conception
of ourselves as decent fellows.

And the short cut to that is to decide that the
impulse which betrayed us was not our own—
that it came from outside ourselves.

"The Serpent beguiled me" is the oldest of all
excuses. We've brought it up to date. We say
that the Jekyll of our normal self has been elbowed
out of the way by some mysterious Hyde for
whom we have no real responsibility.

It is a comforting thought. It restores faith in
that self-portrait of ours. But it isn't so comfortable
to realize that, if Hyde has taken command once,
he may do so again.

Let's try, occasionally, to look at ourselves as
we look at other people. It's not, as a rule,
pleasant. It never is pleasant to have our illusions
shattered. But it may be salutary.

Most of us are neither good nor bad. We are
a strange mixture of strength and weakness, of
noble aspirations and besetting sins.

But we count the aspirations as virtues, even if we never realize them. And we call the besetting sins by gentler names.

A man may have a vile temper. It shadows his home, poisons the relations between himself and his wife, between himself and his children. It makes life hell for his subordinates.

But he very seldom thinks of himself as bad tempered. His outbursts are "justifiable annoyance."

A woman has a cruel tongue. She is constantly saying "catty" things to her friends. Her every sentence is a stab.

Very often she will pride herself on her "frankness."

"I know I am outspoken," she will say. "But it is good for people to hear the truth sometimes."

She never thinks of telling it to herself, of analysing her own shortcomings as mercilessly as those of her neighbours.

We're all, more or less, like that. And the first step we must take if we would really know ourselves is to realize it.

We must learn to call our sins and weaknesses by their right names, to recognize them as sins and weaknesses.

That act of which we were ashamed wasn't something on its own, quite outside the normal current of our lives.

It was something for which we had been preparing. It occurred because of what we are and of what we are becoming.

What we call character isn't something that is fixed and immutable.

It changes gradually, imperceptibly. A thousand little acts, perhaps, to which we have given no heed, went before the one that brought us up with a jerk.

Really, the thing we are so ashamed of is a danger signal. We have been walking towards a precipice, and suddenly a lightning flash has lit up the scene and shown us where we are going.

It's the worst kind of folly to pretend that the flash hasn't happened, or that it has happened to someone else, and to go on as we were doing before.

Every step into sin is easier than the one before. And at last there comes a time when what once we regarded with horror has become a matter of course. We don't say then: "It wasn't I who did it." We have ceased to feel the need of excuses.

But if, when we find ourselves slipping into sin, we face up to the truth about ourselves, smash that false self-portrait and substitute one nearer the reality, we can climb out of the pit we have dug for ourselves.

If every step into sin is easier than the one before, so is every step out of sin. Every time we put temptation behind us, we make the next temptation weaker, and ourselves stronger.

And we do not need to rely upon our own strength alone. Sin comes from within, from a weakness in ourselves. But strength to resist and conquer sin will come to us from without—if we ask for it.

A working man once said to me: "The devil cannot stand against prayer."

It is profoundly true. Prayer, if it is earnest and sincere, will bring new strength always.

God will keep our feet from falling. He will guide us back to the right path.

I HEARD a story the other day of a group of men who were travelling home by train. One of them, in a corner of the carriage, was busy with a crossword puzzle. Suddenly he looked up.

"A word of three letters, with 'o' in the middle meaning man's best friend?" he inquired.

"Dog," chorused everybody. And if you were asked the same question, that's almost certainly the word that would come first to your mind. But it didn't quite fit into the puzzle.

"I think," said the man with the pencil, "that the last letter must be 'd.' "

But still he couldn't see it. And neither apparently could any of his companions. Or, if they did, they didn't like to suggest anything so revolutionary.

Yet surely man's best and most tolerant friend is God.

Probably none of the men in that railway carriage was irreligious. They mightn't go to church very often, they mightn't make any parade of their faith, they might occasionally do things that they knew perfectly well were wrong. But they all called themselves Christians. They all believed in God. And sometimes at least, at crises in their lives, they prayed to Him.

It's always our best friend that we turn to when we're in trouble. We may have been neglecting Him, we may almost have forgotten Him. But, when a real time of testing comes, it is He whom we want by our side.

That applies as between man and man. But there are times when no human friend, however near and dear, can aid us; when those who love us most can only look on helplessly, waiting for the moment when perhaps a word, or a pressure of the hand, can suggest, however inadequately, sympathy and a desire to make things easier for us, and frustration because they know that they cannot.

It is then that we turn to God as a stricken child to its parent. And in nine cases out of ten the prayer that rises to our lips begins: "Our Father which art in Heaven."

Yet, real as we have found this relation to be, as a rule it is kept in the background of our lives. God is the rock to which we flee when we are defeated, or bowed under some great anxiety or grief, not a Companion who journeys with us all the way.

This perhaps is natural enough. Indeed, we feel it to be almost blasphemous when any one claims to be, so to speak, on God's visiting list.

We feel that the person who addresses God too familiarly in prayer, who says over-confidently that God told him to do this or that, is taking His name in vain. We may even suspect him of hypocrisy.

There are hypocrites who, in the words of the old proverb: "Pay tribute to God that they may impose on men."

But there are also large numbers of simple, earnest people whose idea of God is very much that depicted in the film *Green Pastures*. There are differences, no doubt—such differences as one would expect to follow from the difference in race. *Green Pastures* gives us a picture of God and Heaven as they appear to the childlike negro mind.

The white men, of whom I am thinking, looking with other eyes, see another picture. But it is not so very far away in essentials.

God is still a larger edition of themselves or their favourite minister. And they talk to Him, in prayer, as they might talk to that minister.

There is no blasphemy in such a conception of God, or in the sense of familiar communication with the Almighty that flows out of it.

But for many of us it is impossible to think of God in that way. We are too conscious of His Mystery and Majesty. We feel that He is beyond our puny understanding. His thoughts are not our thoughts, nor His ways our ways. And while we call Him Father, we hardly dare to call Him Friend.

At times, it may be, we even hesitate to pray to Him. We look up at the starry heavens, and we think of the innumerable galaxies, the wheeling systems that He created and which obey His will.

In this vast universe, whose limits science continually extends, how small is the globe upon which we live, how insignificant are we.

And how petty, when we think thus, are our troubles and perplexities. What can they matter to God?

Here we reason falsely. We forget the manifestation of God in Jesus Christ.

In a few days we shall commemorate once more the Passion and Death of Our Lord. We shall remember that He died for us—that He knew the bitterness of the Cross so that we should have life—and have it more abundantly.

And on Easter Sunday, we shall greet the Risen Lord.

Christ is God as He has chosen to reveal Himself to us. The Mystery and Majesty remain. But there is added to them an infinite compassion and an infinite love.

We see in Christ God indeed—but God made human, endowed with all the qualities of the Ideal, the Perfect Man. We see also a pattern for ourselves, an example which we may strive to follow.

But the tremendous fact about Jesus Christ is His love. It doesn't matter that we don't deserve it. His love isn't affected by that. He is the one friend we cannot drive away.

The most patient of our fellowmen, however closely he may be bound to us by ties of affection, will only stand so much. But we cannot exhaust the patience of Christ.

We can cut ourselves off from every other human soul. But we cannot cut ourselves off permanently from Christ.

We can break the bonds of blood—alienate for ever our own nearest kin. But we cannot escape the love of Christ. It will haunt us all our days.

Our Lord, while He was on earth, was a Man of Sorrows and acquainted with grief. We can take our sorrows to Him, sure of His understanding. But He rejoiced with the wedding guests at Cana. He will rejoice with us to-day.

Man's best friend is God. But let us remember always that the God Who hung the stars in the heavens, the Lord of the dark immensities of space, is also He Who strengthens the mourners and Who has said: "Suffer little children, and forbid them not, to come unto Me."

We are all, even the best and wisest of us, as little children groping in the dark, and afraid of the dark. His is the Voice that offers to comfort us; His is the Hand that offers to lead us into the light.

SPRING! Time—unless you are an asthmatic —to look out those country shoes and make tracks for downs or moorlands where the air blows free.

Time to return to the woods or the high hills or the cliff paths above the waves. Each to the scenes he has longed for through drab winter days.

All around us Nature renews herself and is glad. The recurrent miracle of spring begins to unfold in a glory of blossom.

Countless generations have hailed this annual rebirth, this triumph of life.

And some at least, in every generation, have looked beyond the thing seen to the thing unseen, and have caught a glimpse in this annual resurrection of nature of the type and symbol of a larger hope.

The first intimations of immortality came to man in the spring. He dared to suspect, foreshadowing the Gospel story, a God who died and who rose again from the dead.

In a sense this was a dramatization of the rhythm of nature. But it was also an expression of man's passionate desire for some assurance of a life beyond the gates of death.

He was as yet groping blindly—feeling his way in darkness. But his face was towards the light.

So the stories of Osiris and Adonis, to mention two of the most famous of the resurrection myths of the ancient world, had a deeper significance than we are accustomed to allow them.

They made men familiar with the idea of immortality. They suggested that death might be, not the end of all, but a bridge between two lives.

In a sense, therefore, it is possible to say that these pagan gods, no less than John the Baptist, prepared the way of the Lord.

Students of comparative religion sometimes deceive themselves; because they are aware of this theme in the old mythologies, and can trace there not only the idea of resurrection, but also the idea of sacrifice, they believe that the Christian revelation can be set aside.

This is not the case. The resurrection of Our Lord, which we celebrate in our churches—and I hope in our hearts also—is to these ancient myths as the noonday to the twilight.

It is the fulfilment, not only of Jewish prophecy, but also of those unconscious prophecies of ancient peoples.

Remember, Christ came, not to the Jews only, but to all the world. The Gentiles also had to be made ready for His coming.

Viewed from this angle, these foreshadowings, like the others which we find in Plato and the great classical philosophers, bear a different aspect.

But—and this is also my answer to those who wrote me asking: "How do you know that Christ is God?"—it is the great central facts of Our Lord's character and teaching that are conclusive.

Osiris and Adonis have left behind them a legend. But they are shadowy figures, moving in a fairy-tale world remote from our experience. They have no substance, no reality to us to-day.

Who among us can say that of Jesus Christ? We know Him better than we know our friends.

He is far more real to us than the people whom we meet every day, with whom we have intimate dealings. And we know that He is unique—that he stands alone—that never, since the beginning of the world, has there been any one with whom we can compare Him.

There have been good men who have also been teachers and leaders in every age and every nation.

But they have all, in some way, failed and fallen short. And we can trace in all of them the influence of the times and of the land in which they lived. We can see the forces that have gone to their making.

We can also see how their teaching has grown out of the circumstances of their lives. And we discern its limitations.

The seers of old, we say, taught such and such because this, in their day, was the vital and important thing. But it is not so vital and important to us to-day. Perhaps it is not even true any longer.

But we refuse to be made alive while we reject the values which Our Lord has proclaimed.

There is a mystical sense in which we must die to the old Adam before we can be made alive in Christ. We must make an end of the tiger within us, that clings to the old brutish codes, before we can become of the company of God.

It is not that God shuts us out. We shut ourselves off from Him. It is not that Christ denies us. We deny Him. And the denial of Christ is, in the end, the suicide of the soul.

I AM getting rather tired of hearing people say: *"But, of course, you parsons take the sentimental view of everything."* They seem to think that sentimentality is the occupational disease of the clergy.

It's nothing of the sort. The parson, like the doctor, lives too close to the great central facts of life and death to be sentimental.

You can't sit by a deathbed and talk empty sentimentality. Life at the last is stripped bare of shams and illusions. Those who are about to die see clear.

You can't be sentimental when you're in the presence of a great bereavement. The words that would be a mockery of sorrow die upon your lips.

And when you marry two young people—or baptise a child? Well, the parson gets to know a good deal about other people's marriages. And he has a pretty shrewd idea of what life has in store for the child.

There are times when I almost wonder how parsons manage to escape being cynical. If they didn't have faith in God, if they didn't have that faith renewed and strengthened by prayer, I am sure they would be so.

154

They see too much. It is the biggest of mistakes to imagine that ministers of religion live sheltered lives.

Many of them have just as hard and grim a struggle against poverty as the underpaid clerk with a mortgage and a family.

Others have to endure incessant intrigues, jealousies and bickerings. There are country parishes that are made little hells for the parson by backbiting and malice. The village is sometimes a loudspeaker.

Even those who escape this have little encouragement for sentimentality. Their own lives may be calm, but they learn a great deal about the storms of others.

Men and women come to them at times of crisis. And they see what life does to the young people they have learned to love—how it hardens and coarsens, or tortures and breaks them.

There is hardly any aspect of the human tragedy that they do not encounter in the course of their job.

A psychologist once told me that there was none of the dark places of the mind of man that was not explored and charted—long before Freud—by the priests of the Catholic Church.

He said that there were old manuals, prepared for the guidance of priests hearing confessions, that were startlingly up-to-date in their descriptions of sick souls and minds diseased.

The Confessional was, in fact, the earliest psychological clinic, and the father confessor was the first psychologist.

Men and women still seek relief from the burden of sin and unhappiness in laying bare their souls to some clergyman. And one of the first things a parson has to learn is not to be shocked—not to drive away the sinner, however much he may hate the sin.

So parsons get to know a great deal—much more, indeed, than they want to know—about the seamy side of human nature. And that makes sentimentality difficult.

Also the average clergyman has been trained to think—and to think clearly. He may not find, in the multiplicity of parochial duties, as much time as he would like for thought, but the training is there. And he can usually detect the false logic of the sentimentalists.

His "hard-hearted" critics are frequently quite unable to do that. Some of the biggest sentimentalists are to be found among the very people who talk about the sentimentality of the clergy.

You can see sentimentality cropping up in all sorts of curious ways and places.

Some years ago a great advocate was defending a woman against whom a serious charge had been brought. In his speech he described the circumstances of her life. Then he paused and turned to the jury with a dramatic gesture.

"Gentlemen," he exclaimed, "*God has never given her a chance. Won't you?*"

The crowded court burst into applause. And
the woman was acquitted.

The appeal came near to sheer blasphemy—and
a moment's thought should have shown its falsity.
But it achieved its purpose.

The sentimental appeal, indeed, is usually
successful—there are so many sentimentalists in
the world.

Why, then, accuse the clergy of sentimentality?

In the main, because the parson stands for a
higher standard of conduct—an inconvenient
standard. One way of evading the demands of
Christianity is to label them as sentimental.

They are nothing of the kind. There is no
sentimentality in declaring man's duty to his
fellow-men and to God.

But it is sentimental to shed tears over a novel
or a film while ignoring the mass of human misery
at our doors.

There is no sentimentality in saying "Thou
shalt not kill." There *is* sentimentality in thinking
of war in terms of swords and shining armour
when it has become an affair of poison gas and
incendiary bombs and the slaughter of women and
children. (But that, unfortunately, is a form of
sentimentality from which even the clergy are not
immune.)

There is no sentimentality in condemning greed,
and envy, and malice, and all uncharitableness.
There *is* sentimentality in pretending that these
things can be eradicated by some political panacea
or economic revolution.

There is no sentimentality in believing that Christianity can save the world. There *is* sentimentality in the delusion that the world is very nice as it is, and doesn't need to be saved.

There is no sentimentality in prayer, and worship, and a humble endeavour to follow in the footsteps of Our Lord.

There *is* sentimentality in calling ourselves Christians, and going to church two or three times a year, or even every Sunday, while we evade the practical obligations of the faith that we profess.

No, it isn't the parsons who are sentimentalists. The sentimentalists are those who busy themselves with shams and shadows, or play with false and artificial emotions, while they shut their eyes to the evil they don't want to see or the duty that might disturb the even tenor of their comfortable lives.

I LIKE the old story of the woman who, after a careful study of the "character" supplied by a prospective maid, looked up and remarked approvingly:

"That is a very nice character." To which the young woman replied:

"I'm glad you like it, ma'am. I wrote it myself."

We could all have very nice "characters" if we wrote them ourselves. But, after all, why not? There would be nearly as much sense in it as there is in the present system.

I have always considered this business of demanding references from servants as too one-sided. And its value as a safeguard is very small. No one who enters another person's household with criminal intentions fails to provide himself—or herself—with excellent references.

Should we demand references from an employee unless we are prepared to give them?

We advertise for a maid, and offer, in addition to wages, "a good home." But girls who apply for the job have to take our description on trust.

We ask them for the names and addresses of their former employers so that we can learn all about them. But we would have ten different kinds of fit if they asked for the name and address of our last maid, so that they might get the "low-down" on us.

Yet that surely would be a fairer way of doing it. Let the employer furnish references as well as the employee.

If we are taking a stranger into our home, and want to be sure that she is the right sort, we are equally strangers to her. Suppose she is a young girl. Isn't she taking a risk in entering a house of which she knows nothing?

We want an assurance that she is good-tempered and courteous, because we find it unpleasant to have a girl who is sulky and surly. But hasn't she just as great an interest in learning what sort of temper we have?

All along the line it is the same. There is nothing that we want to know about her that she hasn't just as much need to know about us.

Even if we admit this, we don't like the idea of a girl we're going to employ getting her first mental picture of us from a former maid.

There have been certain little unpleasantnesses —perhaps it is because of one of these that we are changing our domestic staff. So we feel that the "reference" our late employee would give might not be flattering.

Wait a moment, though. What about the reference we gave her? Was it coloured by those same disagreements? We are afraid this former maid might not be just to us. But have we been just to her?

It begins to look as if we can't accept any of those references at face value. They are worthless unless we know the character of the people who wrote them and the circumstances in which they were written.

The truth is that every personal relation— whether it be that of mistress and maid, husband and wife, or parent and child—is a job for two. Each must do his or her part if it is to be a success.

When it is a failure it is no use merely blaming the other person. The chances are that there are just as many faults on our own side. And it's much more profitable to look for those. Only we can put right what is wrong with ourselves.

And if ours is only one side of the relation, it is the side that is our responsibility. Also in tackling it, we may be helping the other side to get right.

There is common sense as well as Christianity in the injunction: "Do unto others as you would that they should do unto you." The way to get the best out of other people is to give them the best that is in us.

This applies in every field of life. And the reverse is just as true.

We can usually rely on seeing the worst of other people if we show them the worst of ourselves.

So there is something self-revealing in our estimates of our fellow-men. These estimates depend always on how they behave to us. And how they behave to us is often as much our doing as theirs.

When I find a man with a low opinion of human nature I don't ask what other people have done to him. I wonder what he has done to them.

On the other hand, the man who is decent and kindly will tell you that other people are, for the most part, the same. That is his experience. He helps them to be so.

Here's an exercise that might do us all good. Let's do what the young woman did in the story and write our own "character." Only let's do it, not to impress some one else with our value, but to get at the truth about ourselves.

What shall we say? Honest, truthful, hard-working?

Are we always honest? Or do we sometimes ignore the odd coppers when we're paying a tradesman's bill, or keep him waiting for his money, or fail to point out a mistake that is in our favour, or forget to pay excess fare if we travel with the wrong railway ticket?

Truthful? Do we tell the truth when it's unpleasant to ourselves, or only when it's unpleasant to some one else?

Hard-working? Do we put our backs into it just as hard when the chief is looking the other way as we do when he's watching? Aren't there times when we "ca' canny"?

No doubt there are reasons for it. We aren't feeling up to the mark, or the atmosphere is wrong. But other people about whose work we grumble have exactly the same excuses to offer.

Are we easy to get on with? If we find other people difficult we may take it for granted that we are difficult ourselves.

So we may go on, asking all the questions about ourselves that we would ask about any one we meant to employ. Perhaps when we have finished we will be a little more charitable next time we sit in judgment on other people.

Or, better still, we will decide to take ourselves in hand. We can always get rid of a maid who is unsatisfactory—but we can't get rid of ourselves. And our happiness depends far more upon ourselves—upon our own character and temperament —than it does upon any one else.

So let's stop thinking about other people's shortcomings and tackle our own. We're more likely to get results that way.

EARLIER in these pages I had something to say about politicians who lacked moral courage. When a friend read the article in the newspaper where it first appeared, he tackled me about it.

"Honestly," he said, "do you think the rest of us are any better?"

That comes uncomfortably near home. We can get a kick out of condemning politicians, or any other class of people we don't admire, but how far are we justified in feeling superior?

If we do, aren't we in danger of becoming like that Pharisee who thanked God that he was not as other men?

But I'm not sorry I wrote as I did, I'm not going to withdraw anything I said. Though, of course, it might have been said better. Yet there's something in my friend's challenge. Let's look at it. Let's look at ourselves.

There comes a point where we can only keep in step with our friends and neighbours—and perhaps with our family—by giving up something which we believe to be right, or by agreeing, at least tacitly, to something we know to be wrong.

Here comes the test of moral courage. It's easy

enough to do the right thing if everybody else is agreed that it is the right thing.

But it becomes very hard to do it when the booing sets in.

One of the bravest fellows I knew was a lad who worked in a factory. He was a Christian—and he tried to live his Christianity.

That isn't an easy matter at any time, not in even the best of circumstances.

In this case, the youngster's foreman called himself an atheist, and delighted in making him a butt. The rest took their cue from the foreman. They made that boy's life a perfect hell.

I couldn't understand why these likeable men with, presumably, their traditional love of fair play, allowed that persecution to continue and even took part in it themselves.

I concluded, reluctantly, that it was cowardice —that the men wanted to keep in with the foreman and were much afraid of getting out of favour.

I was very young then. Now I know better. Those men weren't cowards in that sense.

They weren't scared for their jobs—and very probably none of them would have minded having a scrap with the foreman.

But each was afraid of something else—afraid that if he stood up for the youngster, or if he refused to join in the baiting, his mates would think he, too, had "got religion."

An Englishman is more ashamed of his virtues than of his faults.

Tell him that he's a bit of a dog, hint at dark

secrets in his past and illicit love affairs now in progress, and he'll be rather pleased.

Tell him his proper place is at a Y.M.C.A. or a prayer meeting, and he'll probably be really annoyed.

A century ago in this country cruelty to children was a commonplace, cruelty to animals was a commonplace, drunkenness was a commonplace.

The people who tried to stop these things were regarded as cranks and sentimentalists. They were laughed at. Sometimes they were even man-handled.

To-day cruelty to children or animals is rare. When it does occur it is almost invariably reported by indignant neighbours.

Drunkenness is a dying vice.

These things aren't fashionable any more. Group opinion has condemned them. But it only did so because, in the first place, a handful of men and women had the moral courage to proclaim a standard that was higher than the general standard of their day, and to range themselves on the minority side for conscience' sake.

How many of us have the guts to do the same sort of thing where to-day's fashionable sins are concerned?

Here's one test. What do you do when somebody tells a dirty story? Do you make any protest —even the silent one of not joining in the guffaws?

Once at a bachelor party an unpleasant young man prefaced the story he was about to tell with this remark: "No ladies present, I think?" "No," said his host, "but there are some gentlemen."

That tale was not told.

It is time that decent people did protest. These stories are spread around much more widely than they used to be.

They are no longer confined to the smoking-room. They are spilling over into mixed companies.

They are poisonous stuff, and unfortunately the young are sometimes inclined, when they hear their elders telling "funny" stories, to think it the manly thing to do—a tip from the masculine stable.

It might be said that this doesn't matter much. It is an age of frankness. But frankness doesn't mean beastliness.

What is the use of telling young people about sex in the right way if, going out into the world, they find everywhere the subject is made an occasion for cheap and nasty witticisms, and coarse and dirty anecdotes?

There are other tests for our moral courage—plenty of them.

But when I talk to eager, clean-minded youngsters, I feel that this one may be particularly vital and important.

These smoking-room stories contaminate the wells of life. They foul the most beautiful things in the world. They bring a furtive look into eyes that should be clear and fresh as the morning. They make men leer, and a leering man is ugly, inside and out.

Have we the courage to face the sneers, the shrugged shoulders, the contemptuous gibes of friends and acquaintances in order to kill this modern dragon and make life cleaner for youth?

If we take a stand here, we needn't think we are fine fellows. To refrain from taking part in what we believe to be harmful and contemptible is nothing, after all, to make a song about.

ABOLISH THE BIRCH

FROM time to time worried parents write to me to ask what they should do with a troublesome child.

They have already had advice—plenty of it. But as half their counsellors recommend a good whipping and the other half say that whipping is brutal and barbarous, they aren't much further forward. So they want to know what I think.

I have never belonged to "the more you beat 'em the better they be" school of thought. But there was a period when I should certainly have said that, in some circumstances, physical correction would benefit the majority of boys.

At the same time I should have added the warning that there were some boys whom it would be wicked to punish in this way. Everyone accustomed to working among young people can recognize such boys, but I don't know if the father of one or two small children could be expected to do so.

To-day I am as convinced as ever that there are youngsters to whom corporal punishment may do tremendous harm. But I'm no longer so sure that there are any to whom it may do good.

Please don't reply that Solomon said: "Spare

the rod and spoil the child." Solomon didn't say it.

And it is doubtful if he was responsible either for the verse in "Proverbs": "He that spareth the rod hateth his son; but he that loveth him chasteneth him betimes." The Book of "Proverbs" is the work of many hands.

In any case, this verse must be read in relation to the manners and customs of the Jews in Old Testament times. They believed in and practised corporal punishment, not only for children, but for grown-up men and women.

The most that can be said is that, to our own knowledge, there are boys who are smacked who grow up to be good men: and there are others who aren't smacked who are selfish and un-pleasant in later life. But it isn't the smacking or the absence of it that is responsible in either case.

What is true, and always will be true, is that the child who grows up in an atmosphere of love and trust and confidence gets a flying start in life.

He is able to face the problems of youth and maturity with courage and good will. He is equipped to find happiness and to keep it.

The man who has had this kind of upbringing doesn't need laws and judges and policemen to keep him in order.

As a rule he does the decent thing, as if by instinct. But it isn't instinct. It is the force and power of example and of love.

Smacking can't add to that—or take away from it. Really it's unnecessary, but the father may not realize that. So he smacks his son when he thinks it is for the boy's own good.

Because of the bond of love and trust between father and son, the smacking does no harm. But it achieves nothing that couldn't have been achieved equally well by other means.

The same thing holds good at school. Wherever there are trust, affection, and respect, physical correction is not required. But if, by tradition and custom, it is retained, there are usually no permanent ill-effects.

There was a period when I was responsible for the good behaviour of hundreds of boys. I had to maintain discipline among them. Much more important, I had to do what I could to make men of them—to help them to build character.

At that time I had hardly begun to think out issues of conduct for myself. I accepted without question the greater part of the public school code in which I had been trained. I believed in corporal punishment—and when I thought it was necessary I administered it.

But—I never allowed a boy to go away afterwards feeling angry and resentful. After it was over we'd have a cup of tea and a game of draughts or chess together. And we'd part good friends.

I can honestly say that I do not think I ever lost a friend as a result of one of those incidents. But looking back, I consider that is more to the boys' credit than to mine.

At the moment, the birching of juvenile law-

breakers is very much under discussion. This, of
course, is in quite a different category to a home
correction, but it is sometimes defended on the
ground that boys are birched at public schools,
and what is good enough for a young duke should
be good enough for a young delinquent.

I wonder if perhaps it might be useful to
consider this special problem in the light of what
we have just been saying on the general question
of corporal punishment.

We have agreed—or I hope we have agreed—
that the important thing is the relation between
the child and the adults who are responsible for
his training. If that relation is right, even if
physical correction does no good, at least it doesn't
do any serious harm.

And sometimes it may seem to do good. If a
boy has been in the care of someone who, while
he punished in the traditional way, still knew how
to inspire trust and affection, he is apt, when he
grows up, to give part of the credit for his successful
upbringing to the whippings he received.

Similarly, if corporal punishment is a recognized
and normal part of a system of education—like
that of our public schools—which, on the whole,
turns out decent and honourable men, those
educated in this way will tend to regard it as
healthy and wholesome.

That explains why so many kindly, intelligent
men—M.P.'s and magistrates—want to retain
the birch as a punishment. They believe that
birching is useful and salutary in the public

schools. Therefore, they argue, it must be good in the police court.

But a police-court whipping isn't normal. And there is no personal relation between the boy who receives it and the men who inflict it.

Both the magistrate who orders the birch and the police officer who lays it on are impersonal representatives of the law. There is no bond of sympathy or understanding between them and the boy.

He may find a certain compensation in the awe with which some of his schoolfellows regard him. Because of the unnatural atmosphere of the whole business, he is able to pose as a hero. But if he is to maintain this pose he must "do it again"— he mustn't allow it to seem that he has been deterred or intimidated by the birch.

That's how criminals are made—how youngsters are turned into enemies of society.

The boy who is birched is an outcast. But he's a fine fellow because he has broken the law, been punished in a spectacular way, and still goes on in defiance of magistrates and policemen and birch rods.

This is hopeless.

What we want is to make the youngster feel that he's a fine fellow, not because he has done wrong, but in spite of it. Until we can accomplish that we will go on making criminals.

There is one way in which we can wipe out immediately the larger part of juvenile delinquency and its present disastrous consequences.

That is to take out of the hands of the courts altogether all but the most serious cases of offences by children. Let the schools deal with them.

They used to do so. I am told that nine out of ten of the offences which are now handled by magistrates, probation officers and policemen were, a few years ago, regarded as the business of headmasters.

Let them go back to the schools. The relation between a boy and his headmaster is a human and personal relation.

Even if the head believes in corporal punishment, at least his correction will not leave the same scars on the soul that the police-court birching does. As for the boys who would still be dealt with by the courts—those who commit the ten per cent. of more serious offences—they might, I think, benefit far more from skilled psychological treatment than from the birch.

Such treatment has been tried in apparently hopeless cases with remarkable results.

On the wider, general question, may I say just one word more? Beating a boy doesn't drive the "wickedness" out of him. It may drive it in.

The thing that makes a boy into a good man is the example of parents and teachers. If their behaviour sets the right pattern, and they know how to win the youngster's affection and trust, corporal punishment is unnecessary.

If, on the other hand, they can't inspire confidence and love, corporal punishment is vicious and harmful.

SLAY YOUR DRAGON

ENGLISHMEN don't make much fuss about
their patron saint. April 23, indeed, is as
much Shakespeare's day as St. George's.

There is no one who thus shares the honours
with St. Andrew, or St. David, or St. Patrick.
But we are, quietly, just as proud of our saint as
any Scot, or Welshman, or Irishman is of his.

And why shouldn't we be? He is a fine, romantic figure—this martyr for his faith who slew the
dragon. Naturally, we refuse to believe that
malicious story of Gibbon's, which makes him a
mere seller of bacon, however appropriate such
a patron saint might be to a "nation of shopkeepers."

Of course, Napoleon misjudged us. We English
are "romantics" at heart. We may spend our
working life selling groceries behind a counter, or
totting up figures in a ledger.

It doesn't matter. We have day-dreams of
tropic seas and Arctic wastes. We also would go
out and slay dragons, if only we could get the
chance.

Alas, there are no more dragons.

Aren't there?

There are, perhaps, no creatures exactly like

those on the gold coins we don't see any longer nowadays. Nevertheless, our modern world contains a good many dragons—bigger, fiercer, harder to kill than the one which St. George overthrew.

The fight against dragons is, indeed, a never-ending one.

You remember the description of the seven-headed monster in the Revelation of St. John the Divine, and how "Michael and his angels fought against the dragon, and the dragon fought and his angels."

You remember how, in the "Pilgrim's Progress," Christian met Apollyon in the Valley of Humiliation. There was a good deal of the dragon about Apollyon.

"The monster," says Bunyan, "was hideous to behold; he was clothed with scales like a fish, and they are his pride; he had wings like a dragon, feet like a bear, and out of his belly came fire and smoke; and his mouth was as the mouth of a lion."

There are differences, but in essence Apollyon is the dragon of Revelation, and the dragon of St. George—and our own particular dragon, which we are called upon to deal with. The battle against dragons is the battle against evil.

It is a battle to which we are called.

Centuries ago, when our ancestors faced desperate odds, their rallying cry was "St. George for Merrie England!" Among the dragons we must tackle are those which have turned "Merrie

England" into a place of suffering and despair for so many.

It is a mockery to talk of "Merrie England" to the men and women of the depressed areas, who have known for so long the sickness of hope deferred. There is no "Merrie England" for them—only the slow starvation of the dole, less adequate to human needs than ever now that bread, the staple food of the poor, has been increased in price.

What are we doing about the dragon of unemployment, which has laid waste the homes of these unfortunate folk?

I am afraid we are doing what the cowards of every age and every land have done with dragons —what the people of Silene did with theirs until St. George came along to deliver them. We are saying:—

"Now be a good dragon and stay where you are. We'll give you some of our best men and women to feed on—as many as any reasonable dragon can want—so long as you stay quietly out of sight and leave the rest of us alone."

Surely a great nation, that has chosen St. George as its patron saint, that has at its command all the resources of modern science, can devise a better way than this of dealing with the dragon of unemployment.

Then there are many who have escaped unemployment for the moment, but who are still in the grip of the dragon of poverty.

Think of all the agricultural labourers who are

trying to bring up a family on thirty shillings or so a week.

Think of all the town workers who believed that a new world was opening to them when they secured a house on a council estate—or perhaps bought a home of their own on mortgage—and now find that they have to cut down on food in order to pay the higher rents or the building society instalments.

Again, this is a quiet dragon. As a rule, we don't see him unless we go out to look for him. But he is feeding upon the people just the same.

Is there nothing we can do about him except go on pretending he isn't there?

And there is another dragon—perhaps the most terrible of all—who may even now be getting ready to spring upon us. The dragon of war.

Even without taking into account the various lesser dragons most of us could name, there would seem to be a man-sized job waiting for any experienced dragon-killer who liked to apply. But I'm afraid St. Georges are rather rare to-day. If we want to get rid of our dragons we shall have to tackle them ourselves.

Shall we take a vow on England's day and St. George's—each of us to do what he can for the sake of the land we love?

But if we are to make England the country she might and ought to be, we must face and conquer the dragon within ourselves.

In all of us there is some strain of weakness, some darling sin. We must not forget this personal dragon. It may seem tiny and insignificant, hardly worth bothering about. But it will thwart and hamper us at every turn in our fight against its big brothers.

Here then is a twofold task—dragons without and dragons within to tackle. The struggle will be hard. But it is well worth winning.

WALKING along the Strand one evening, I saw one of the Empire soldiers who have come over for the Coronation.

He was a splendid specimen of young manhood, with a frank, open face. But it was clouded when I encountered him. He was in difficulties.

A girl was hanging on to his arm and would not let go. He looked profoundly uncomfortable and unhappy—but he could not shake her off.

As I passed his eyes met mine. There was an unconscious appeal in them.

I walked up to the pair.

"Do you want this lady?" I asked him.

"I do not," he replied.

"Right," I said, and turned to the girl. "Buzz off, my child," I told her. There are occasions when one can't stand on ceremony.

That little incident set me thinking.

From the ends of the earth people are coming to London for the crowning of our King. What sort of welcome are we giving them? How are they going to think of England?

Are we showing them the best that is in our country and ourselves?

I have heard some shameful stories of Coronation profiteering—or attempted profiteering.

They left a bad taste in my mouth—they must have done the same to those who were the victims.

If they have never been over here before, their impressions of us must be bitter and unpleasant.

Such cases are doubtless exceptional. At least I hope that they are exceptional. But when even quite a small stone is cast into a pool, the ripples from it seem to widen out endlessly.

On the whole, however, private visitors from overseas will probably get a square deal.

And before they return they may be able to see, not only the pomp and pageantry of our Coronation procession, but also something of the quiet beauty of our countryside, with its May greenery and old-world villages.

But I am thinking more of those who, like that Empire soldier, have come over on duty. There are many other young men like him. What memories are they to take back with them?

Many of them are being mobbed by empty-headed girls, out for what they call "a good time" and careless how they secure it.

They are being pestered and importuned by women whose trade is vice and whose destiny—perhaps already fulfilled—is disease.

Is it easy to say "No"?

It is easy for you and me, with the background of our homes and our thousand and one interests, our worldly wisdom—and, perhaps, our developed sense of Christian duty.

But it may not be so easy for a young man,

unaccustomed to cities, with little experience of life, and far from home and loved ones.

There are times, too, when the restraints of prudence and morality are loosened—when temptation is seen through the rosy mist of alcohol.

I am told that there are far more teetotallers in the Army to-day than ever before—and that, no doubt, is true of the Empire contingents as well as of the other troops who are in London for the Coronation.

And I know that those who are not teetotallers may yet be very far from being drunkards.

But I am not talking about drunkenness.

I am talking about the slight exhilaration, the optimism, the inclination to "chance it," to take risks, which may be produced by even a moderate amount of alcohol.

So I sincerely hope that our hospitality to Empire soldiers, or to any of the others who are now in London, is not going to take the form of encouraging them to "drink up and have another."

Remember the harpies who may be lying in wait for them outside.

Far better, if you meet one of those young men, and want to be hospitable, ask him home to supper.

Show him what is, I feel, the best and most characteristically English thing in our country—a happy home.

But it would be as well to let your wife know in advance—or there might be a slight cloud over the happiness and he wouldn't get the home atmosphere at its best!

I do feel, however, that we ought to do what we can to give these young men something better to take away from the Empire's capital at this time of dedication than the memory of rapacious gold-diggers.

We cannot, perhaps, do so very much individually—but we could all do little things, and these little things would all mount up.

Many of these Coronation guests of ours would like to see London properly—and don't know where to begin.

There are societies that have, as their purpose, exploring London, which could take parties of men round to places they would otherwise never see—perhaps might never hear of at all.

Even if we aren't members of any such organization, we may still know at least a bit of London well enough to take one soldier, or a couple of soldiers, round.

Or we can take men to the pictures, or to a theatre, or—as I have already suggested—ask them home.

An afternoon on the river or, for those of us who have cars, a run into the country, now at its most delightful—these are other possibilities.

None of these things need cost a great deal of money. It isn't the money that counts anyway.

If we all resolved to do what we could, when we met any of those men, to show them that they were welcome, to extend the hand of fellowship to them, to help them to discover the charm and beauty of our City and our country, then these days of Coronation might be made more memorable still, not only for them, but for ourselves.

More than any of the rest, these young men are our coronation guests. Hospitality should be of the kind that leaves only happy memories.

WHY SO BORED?

THERE is a reaction after every great event. We can't stay up on the heights, live at high pressure all the time. If we do it for a period we inevitably come down "flop" afterwards.

That is true both of national events and of the more personal things that happen to ourselves. But it is mainly, I think, personal.

At the moment, if it weren't for the Whitsun holiday, which has come along to let us down lightly, we'd all be feeling rather deflated.

Still, we do have Whitsun, and we aren't worrying overmuch about how we shall feel on Tuesday morning, when we must get back to work again, with nothing to look forward to but a summer holiday which, perhaps, will seem too far away to count.

After all, life is, or can be, full, even when there is no holiday or public festival. For many of us, indeed, it appears more full than ever before.

There are two things that make a full life— outward circumstances and our own inner resources. And the first isn't much good without the second.

Otherwise, a great many of us would be happier than we are.

We shall be out in the open this Whitsun—at the seaside or in the country. We shall see holiday crowds. We shall encounter bands of hikers swinging along country lanes; we shall meet cyclists everywhere.

We shall probably conclude that there are far too many cars on the road for comfort.

All through the summer these hikers and cyclists and motorists will be exploring Britain in a way that was undreamed of a generation or so ago. A good many of them will go abroad.

It's a splendid thing. All these people are getting a richer, more varied experience.

Every evening, throughout the summer, you will see young men and women playing tennis and other games in parks, and playing-fields, and recreation-grounds.

Progressive public authorities cater specially for these things nowadays. A great many big business concerns have their own sports clubs.

These, too, are comparatively recent developments. One of the things that have made them possible is that extra hour of daylight which we now enjoy from April to the beginning of October.

The Daylight Saving Act, by the way, comes of age at Whitsun. It will then be just twenty-one years since it was passed into law.

Here, I think, is a birthday which our young people, to whom it has meant so much, should celebrate.

But I wonder how many of them have even heard of William Willett, who struggled so long and so hard for this reform, and died before it was placed on the Statute-book.

Then there is wireless, which brings entertainment—and more than entertainment if we don't switch it off—to our own homes.

What an enrichment of life that has made possible.

I could go on adding to this list for quite a long time—and so, I expect, could you.

Yet I seem to meet more people—young people especially—who are bored and discontented than I did twenty-five years ago.

So we come back to the second—and more important—of the two factors that make a full life, our own inner resources.

I'm afraid that we've tended rather to neglect these. In a way, that is nothing to be surprised at —there has been so much outside ourselves to claim our attention.

But it's a mistake. You see, we can't get out of outside things more than we have prepared ourselves to receive.

We may walk, or cycle, or drive a car through all the beauty spots of Britain, or all the finest scenery on the Continent. But if we can't get a thrill from the irises in our own garden at home, or the sunset flaming down into Farmer Jones's field, or the crescent moon swimming up from a cloudbank above a London street, we'll get nothing out of our travels but stiff joints and headaches.

It's no use going away because we are bored at home.

If we are bored at home we shall be bored everywhere.

For we carry our boredom with us. It's a part of ourselves.

So we needn't be surprised when we get it back, a familiar echo, from completely new surroundings.

I read an anecdote of King George V in the correspondence columns of a famous newspaper recently.

He had attended a dinner at one of the Inns of Court. Next him, because of seniority, was placed a venerable Bencher.

This gentleman brought out his best story to amuse the King. It was quite a good story.

But before dinner was over he had told it three times. Then King George decided to make an experiment.

He told the same story to the Bencher.

He was rewarded by a startled exclamation. "Bless my soul, sir!" cried the old lawyer, "now who could have told you that story?"

That sort of thing happens to us all through life. We get back what we give—and never realize the connexion between the two.

Why not tackle our inner resources?

Let us learn to be independent of time and place and circumstance, to be happy with what we have and interested in whatever is nearest to hand.

Above all, let us try to recapture the virtue of quietness, set aside some little time for thought.

We are bored when there is "nothing to do" because we feel aggrieved that, for the moment, there is nowhere to rush to, nothing to claim our attention.

So we are "at a loose end." For the moment life seems empty.

It is empty because there is nothing coming into it from outside and because, accustomed to rely on external things, we have allowed it to remain shallow.

But suppose we use those hours which we have free to strike down within ourselves—down to those deeps of personality, to the soul, that all this time has lain imprisoned.

We release a spring which wells up from within —a spring which never fails. Life is full once more—and remains full. For we have given it depth.

That is what, more than anything, we lack to-day.

Without depth in ourselves, all the rest can help us very little, means very little to us.

With it, all this enrichment of life which modern conditions make possible is given a new value.

We can appreciate and enjoy it as it deserves.

DO you remember the first Armistice Day? Of course you do if you were old enough to be conscious of your surroundings.

It was probably the most moving and memorable day of your life.

At St. Martin-in-the-Fields we had received news of the Armistice in advance, and when the maroons started I was putting notices round the church asking all who wished to join in thanksgiving to come inside.

Many people, we knew, would be glad to take part in a simple service of praise and prayer. But we were not prepared for so overwhelming a response. For nearly twenty-four hours on end we gave thanks and sang hymns.

There was no interval longer than the time necessary for one crowd to leave and another to come in.

We sang simple, familiar hymns in which all could join; we poured out our hearts in gratitude and gladness. But we did not forget—how could we forget?—those whose voices were still for ever.

There was none in all these throngs who did not mourn some near and dear one—husband, son, lover, brother, or familiar friend.

Some were still bowed under a recent bereavement; perhaps it was only a few weeks—or even days—since the news had come which seemed to extinguish the light of life. But though their tears might fall, they still gave thanks—thanks for those who were still spared; thanks for the others who would not now have to suffer as they had suffered.

That was nineteen years ago. Grief in many cases, but by no means in all, has been softened by time. But we do not forget. For some, indeed, there can be no forgetting.

How many women who had thought to make Life's pilgrimage happily, hand in hand with their men, have trod a lonely road for twenty or more years, and must tread it until the end.

So when the eleventh hour of the eleventh day of the eleventh month comes round—St. Martin's Day, as it is known in the calendar—we all pause in our tasks—and there come back, across the widening gulf of years, memories of pride and heartbreak.

But in those intervening years a new generation has grown up, and no boy or girl in school to-day was alive in 1918. There will be many young men and women in the streets and in the churches this Armistice-tide to whom the war is only the vaguest and most unsubstantial of childhood recollections.

They will stand silent with us when the maroons sound. In the two minutes when, for us, Time sweeps back, they will think their own thoughts, far-ranging thoughts, perhaps, but not personal as ours will be.

War to them is only a name, and those who sleep in Flanders, or Gallipoli, or wherever else our dead lie buried, are figures of imagination merely, not the men of flesh and blood whom we remember.

Yet, in that two minutes' hush, when the tides of traffic cease, and the pulse of the machines is stilled, and the whole world waits as for a sign, these young people are very near to us, and we to them.

We recall those who were once as young, as alert, as vital as they are—they feel the power and solemn beauty of the moment, and are made sharers, intuitively, in our mood.

Words cannot bridge the gulf between us and them, but the Silence does.

It seems to bind us all, old and young—those to whom the glory and the splendour of life are in the past, and those for whom they still lie ahead—into a mystical unity.

We feel a sense of comradeship with the living while we remember the noble comradeship of the dead.

That, I think, is the thing that lives in our memory most vividly—the comradeship of those who have passed over, how they laughed with us, sorrowed with us, shared with us in all things.

"He was my pal," a soldier once said to me, telling of the death of his friend. "He'd have given me his last fag."

We remember, then, a great company of com-

rades—men who would have given their last
cigarette to a friend.

You may wonder why I, a notorious and unre-
pentant pacifist, write thus. But Armistice Day
is the one day of the year when I don't want to
talk pacifism, because I do not want to jar by
controversy the mood of those who mourn. And
in our remembrance of the fallen there need be
no glorification of war. Far from it, for we
remember and regret those whom war destroyed
and the splendid friendships it cut short.

In all the belligerent countries of 1914-18, even
where the anniversary is not officially observed,
men and women will be thinking the same
thoughts on the same day.

They will remember the war, as we do, not as
a time of hatred and killing, but as a time of
comradeship.

They will mourn, as we do, "the unreturning
brave."

They will think, as we do, of chairs that have
stood empty these nineteen years or more.

While such remains the mood, here and overseas, on Armistice Day, there is hope for the
world—hope that, in spite of all things, peace may
endure, that these young people, who share our
tribute to the fallen, may not march out upon the
same grim paths, their morning glory be quenched
in the same deep waters.

For comradeship can transcend frontiers and
alliances. It extends to those we once called our
enemies, and there have been many recent events

to show that this sense of a common fellowship is felt in their lands as in ours.

If it rested with the ex-Service Men of all nations, we could be assured that there would never be another European war.

But in all countries a new generation is pressing at the heels of the men of 1914-18.

We feel that on Armistice Day many of these young people share, imaginatively and intuitively, our sense of comradeship with the dead who were our friends. Can they be made partakers in this wider comradeship as well?

I do not know—but I believe in the young. And on Armistice Day, while we remember the dead who died too soon, let us pray also for the youth of the world to-day, that the cup of war may pass from them, and that the path before them may be the path of peace.

"WHAT'S the good of all these conferences?" I once asked a journalist who seemed to spend his life going from one to another of them.

"Oh!" he said; "it's always nice to feel that you're saving the world—or your own little bit of it."

I was reminded of that when I read about the Conservative and Labour Party conferences. I think of it besides when I hear the latest news from Geneva.

And yet, in spite of it all, the world is by no means saved. It is just staggering along, dodging each abyss by the skin of its teeth. Perhaps conferences—or at least conferences as we know them—are not the best way of saving the world after all.

At conferences there is too much temptation to try for results that will look well rather than results that will wear well. Those who attend them play to the gallery.

They think more of how their speeches will be reported in the Press than of the good they may do—or hinder. There is a perpetual striving after effect.

There is no progress along those lines.

It's like children playing games. So long as they

are being watched they don't get on properly with the game: they are too busy "showing off."

When you turn away the game proceeds according to plan. There's a good deal of this child mentality among politicians. And, unfortunately, once they get into positions of responsibility, there's always somebody looking on. So the showing-off hardens into a habit, and the habit becomes second nature.

Even so, if you can manage to get them away from the limelight, they are usually reasonable enough.

George Lansbury, who knows more of them than I do, and has seen them at closer quarters, has a theory that if only six men of good will, able to speak for the six biggest world Powers, were dumped on a desert island, with no experts and no reporters to sidetrack them, they could settle all our most dangerous international problems in a week.

He thinks that they could lay the foundation of enduring peace, and would do so.

I am pretty sure he's right.

Unfortunately, conferences are not held on desert islands, nor are they confined to men of good will and noble purpose. As a rule, they take place in big cities, with an army of Press photographers in attendance, and reel cameramen dashing about frantically, trying to get "shots" of all the celebrities present, not to mention the camp followers, some of whom are pretty nasty bits of work.

The place is stiff with reporters eager for the "dramatic moments" and "highlights" of each day's proceedings.

I am not blaming the Press. The press-men are only doing their job. They would far rather have solid results than petty vanities and squabbles to chronicle. It would be bigger news.

But the reporters represent an unseen audience —and each member of the conference is generally concerned to impress that audience with the belief that its own particular passions and prejudices have been his main concern.

They do not merely want to impress—they want to please. In democratic countries they want to win votes. As a result, far too often they attempt to reconcile irreconcilable positions, to run with the hare and hunt with the hounds.

So you get the Labour Party leaders, for instance, making desperate efforts to find an umbrella big enough, and with a sufficient variety of colours in its fabric, to offer shelter at once to pacifists, class-warriors, collective security enthusiasts and the supporters of rearmament.

That makes politics something between a conjuring trick and an acrobatic performance. Or, if you prefer to put it another way, it is a kind of thimble-rigging. You think you know what has happened to the pea, but you don't.

I am old enough to remember when politics were something different. There were crusaders in the House of Commons when I was young.

Parties stood for Principles. There was reality in politics then: now, there seems hardly any at all.

It looks as if the principles of the politicans are merely the stuff that perorations are made of.

No public man can be really big unless he stands for something bigger than himself, something for which he is prepared to risk his career—in other words, for a principle. The man without a creed in public affairs is nothing but a public danger.

With one or two exceptions we have only little men at Westminster because, in politics to-day, there are no great causes, no principles held to unswervingly through every varying wind of circumstance and popular opinion.

Yet outside the political arena great causes are taking shape. As yet we do not hear much about them at conferences in Parliament. They aren't "practical politics."

My word, I am fed up with the so-called practical man. His record is not creditable; his stock is down.

It was the practical man who promised us a war to end war; it was the practical man who spoke of a world fit for heroes; it was the practical man who made the Treaty of Versailles; it is the practical man who tells us now that if we arm to the teeth there will never be another war—at least, not in his time. It is the practical man . . . but need I continue?

One thing I am certain of: sooner or later—and perhaps quite soon—the people of this country, and of other countries as well, are going to be faced with a great alternative.

Two thousand years ago the Founder of Christianity laid down certain simple rules of human conduct. Some try to act upon those rules in their private life, but there has been no attempt to apply them fully in public life.

Yet I am sure that a very large number of people who before the war had very little use for Christianity have only to sit down and analyse their own deepest experience in recent years, and follow out its lessons to their logical conclusions, in order to find themselves brought by force of circumstances to precisely the Christian philosophy of life; not necessarily in any of its orthodox editions, but in all the severity and richness which Christ Himself gave to it by His life and death, as well as by His words.

Frankly, I see no way of saving the world other than Our Lord's. I believe the big political issue of the next few years will be whether or not we are going to try to make Christianity work, not only in our homes, but outside them, in relation to our neighbours, our fellow-countrymen, and the general body of our fellow-men throughout the world. (If you scoff at that, for pity's sake tell me what *you* propose.)

I know there will be all sorts of difficulties. And it is pretty sure there will be many remarks about the absurdity of running a country on Christian lines.

14

I do not think the situation is hopeless. Christ made demands on men that presupposed high standards of conduct, neighbourliness and personal integrity. Men will often acquiesce in low standards, but they don't like doing it.

Show them the highest and they will do a great deal to attain it, as the climbers did in their efforts to conquer Everest.

Our Everest, like theirs, may defy us. But at least we can start climbing. And I think that the great majority of people are far more ready than some politicians and "practical men" imagine to begin the steep ascent. They know that the air will be purer higher up.

ANY one who publicly expresses an opinion on the affairs of the day is liable to be "shot at" by those who don't like his views.

In my time I have said what I think about a good many questions, and have come in for a considerable amount of criticism in consequence. As a rule, I don't complain.

An attack has been made upon me, however, which I feel that I cannot let pass in silence. Some time ago I wrote an article on the Marriage Bill and the attitude of the Church towards divorce and the re-marriage of divorced persons.

Speaking in the House of Commons, Commander Bower, M.P. for Cleveland, suggested that this article was *a betrayal of Christ*.

I cannot place any other interpretation on his remarks:

> "I cannot help wondering how much that pillar of the Church received for that article. I should like to know the exact number of pieces of silver."

I do not know how much of the article Commander Bower read, or how carefully he read it. But there does not seem to me to be one single word in it which could justify such an accusation.

It expresses honest opinions, honestly held—
opinions which, moreover, are held by many other
clergymen of the Church of England, and have
been put on record by them. Nor is there anything in it that appears to me contrary to the
spirit of Our Lord.

May I say just one word more on this aspect of
the subject? The theme of the article was not
suggested to me.

I wrote as I did because, on the whole, I believe,
with Mr. A. P. Herbert, that the Marriage Bill
is "a Christian Bill," and I considered it my duty
to lend it what support I could.

I had also, however, another motive. I wished
to protest against the dropping from the Bill of the
conciliation proposals which it originally contained, and to suggest that they should be restored.
I must confess that I can see nothing in that
which is un-Christian or unworthy.

So much for the personal side. I turn to something which, although it may have been intended
in a personal sense, has a more general bearing.

Commander Bower spoke of "that most ghastly
of present-day phenomena, the journalist-Churchman."

He has a curious sense of proportion. Whatever
one may think of "the journalist-Churchman,"
there are surely many more ghastly phenomena in
the world.

There is the misery of long-continued unemployment, which still holds the depressed areas in
its cruel grip.

There are the thousands of under-nourished children, with their pinched, wan faces.

There are all the other evils that spring from poverty and want.

There are "envy and malice and all uncharitableness." There is injustice, the cruelty of man to man. There is racial persecution. There is the horror of war.

But perhaps I take a picturesque phrase too literally. Doubtless all that Commander Bower intended to convey was that he did not like "the journalist-Churchman."

Why not? Does he think it undignified for a parson to write for the Press? Does he believe that a clergyman should stick to the pulpit—or that he must be neglecting his proper job if he contributes to a newspaper?

The parson's job, as I see it, is to make the message of Christianity known as widely as he possibly can. I do not think he is doing that adequately by preaching to the people—be they many or few—who happen to come to church.

There are many who do not come to church—some of them because, by reason of age or illness, they cannot; others because they feel that the Church has nothing to give them; others because they "just don't bother about religion."

There is not a parson in the country who does not realize that these non-churchgoers are, in a sense, his responsibility; who would not like, if he could, to take the Christian message to them.

Each of us must tackle the problem in his own

way. But of one thing I am convinced. None of us is entitled to ignore whatever opportunities may come to him if it is humanly possible to take them.

Why should the newspaper be ruled out as a method of approach?

The Press is the forum of democracy. It is, as Disraeli called it, "The Fourth Estate."

It exercises a great, and sometimes a decisive, influence upon public opinion.

There may be times when its power is misused. But, upon the whole, the record of the newspapers of this country, at any rate, is an honourable one.

To the freedom of the Press we owe the exposure of many wrongs and abuses; its vigilance is one of the surest safeguards of our freedom; we are indebted to it for the triumph of many good causes.

I see nothing, therefore, of which to be ashamed in being a contributor to a newspaper. And articles dealing with some aspect of religion in a human, informal way, or relating some modern problem to Christian principles, may be a means of reaching many men and women who otherwise have no point of contact with the Church.

It may, of course, be the offence of the "journalist-Churchman" that he is not content to write in a purely abstract manner—that from time to time he refers to controversial topics, and expresses views on matters which have a political bearing.

But if there is any reality in Christianity, it must be related to every sphere of human activity. It is not enough to accept Christian teaching as something in which we believe.

We must apply it, as far as we can, to our lives.

We must use it as a touchstone in public as well as in private affairs.

Often we will be painfully conscious of falling short of the Christian ideal. But that isn't a reason for throwing up the sponge. It is rather a signal for renewed effort.

The Church has no politics, and I believe that Churchmen should not concern themselves in the struggles of political parties.

But that is not to say that they must not concern themselves with social questions, or that they should be silent in the presence of social evils.

Then there is the question of dignity. The Bishop of London said the other day that, when the Church Army was founded, the Church was "dying of dignity."

There are times when I am afraid that the disease persists and the patient is still on the danger list.

But in all the Churches there are parsons who are deciding that, if dignity is going to hamper the spreading of the Gospel of Christ, then dignity must be sacrificed.

It is not so important as human souls.

How to reach the people, and especially those who are careless and indifferent—that is the problem of the Churches to-day.

We must find an answer to it. It is a subject so

urgent, so vitally important, that I propose to
return to it.

But meantime I would say this:

"It is a good thing that religion should be discussed in the Press. It is a good thing that the
everyday problems of men and women, and the
great social questions of our time, should be
brought, in the columns of great newspapers, to
the touchstone of Christianity."

St. Paul, when he set out to carry the Christian
message, sought out the people of the cities he
visited in the places where they congregated for
discussion.

Perhaps the most notable modern equivalent of
those popular forums of the ancients is the Press.

I cannot help thinking that, had he lived to-
day, St. Paul might have been another—and
the greatest—of those journalist-Churchmen Commander Bower so much dislikes.

A COMPETENT official in the Indian Civil Service was "ticking off" an Indian who occupied a fairly responsible post.

"Why didn't you use your imagination, man?" he demanded.

"Sir," came the reply, "I have no imagination, only technical knowledge."

An Englishman, in similar circumstances, might not have been equally frank. But there are quite a number of Englishmen—and others—who are in very much the same position as that Indian.

No one has ever taught them to cultivate, or to use, their imagination. And because of that, their technical knowledge may lose much of its value, and even become positively dangerous.

All over the world we find dull, pompous men without imagination occupying key positions— and there has never been a time in history when this saving gift has been more necessary.

What do I mean by imagination?

I mean the faculty that enables us to see the possible consequences of our actions at several removes.

I mean the quality of sympathetic understanding that enables us to get inside the other fellow's skin, to visualize his life, to see with his eyes, think as he thinks, feel as he feels.

There is no reason why this shouldn't co-exist with technical knowledge. But, as a general rule, it doesn't.

Let's take a concrete illustration. There are men who think in figures, who see every problem in terms of a mathematical equation, or a neatly plotted graph on squared paper.

Set them to work on unemployment. They will produce all sorts of elaborate statistics about it. They will tell us how to keep the Unemployment Fund solvent.

They will work out the probable course of unemployment over a period of years, how much it will cost in benefit, what contributions will be necessary, and so on.

It is all very useful and necessary.

But they will be so absorbed in the figures that they will forget the men and women these figures represent.

If the figures have been reduced to "manageable" proportions, if the Insurance Fund is solvent—that will seem to them sufficient.

They won't bother about the people who are still without work and without hope.

They won't bother because they never think about these people. They never use imagination to create a picture of what unemployment means.

They cannot conceive of themselves, or any one like them, as belonging to that legion of despair.

That is true, I think, not only of a good many civil servants, but also of M.P.s and Ministers.

It almost seems as if, the more familiar they are with figures, the more easily they find their way about in mazes of statistics, the further away they get from the realities these things represent.

So there is all too much truth in what the Bishop of Ely said not long ago, in commenting on our 1,300,000 registered unemployed: "The great tragedy of this for the best man seems to be that he is conscious that he is not wanted; that the State has no use for him and has very little regard for him; that he is hardly a person, but only a statistic."

It isn't only the statisticians who make him feel like that. It is the officials who work by rule and routine, who interpret regulations blindly, and strangle humanity with red tape.

I have received innumerable complaints of the treatment meted out to unemployed men. "You'd hardly think we were human beings at all," wrote one of them.

"You'd almost think they enjoyed knocking us off benefit," wrote another.

"And all the time they seem to think we're trying to do them."

Yet no doubt the officials are kindly men. But many of them have to work against time.

And the regulations which bind them appear to be framed, in the main, by those who regard the unemployed man merely as a statistic, and only take human nature into account in so far as it may be liable to "swing the lead" if it isn't watched.

I may be told that all this is grossly unfair. Human needs are considered. And in the depressed areas public money has been made available to provide work.

Training centres have been established. All sorts of schemes have been set on foot.

But isn't the habit of mind behind this defence exactly the habit of mind we're considering?

Any one who knows the depressed areas knows perfectly well that the sums of money made available are totally inadequate, that the various schemes which look so well on paper barely touch the fringe of the problem.

But figures can be given—and the figures hypnotize us into the belief that something is being done.

Actually, the best and most useful work in the depressed areas has been done by groups of people with comparatively little money—but with imagination and sympathy.

The human touch, contributed by these groups, has accomplished far more for South Wales, for instance, than successive Governments.

Take another illustration.

We hear a great deal about the housing estates which have been built during recent years. We've been applauding slum clearance schemes.

But the technical efficiency which has rehoused

so many of our people might, with advantage, have been mixed with a little more imagination.

There is a serious weakness in connexion with some of those schemes.

Even allowing for subsidies, the rents of houses on the new estates are usually higher—and may be considerably higher—than those paid for old slum dwellings.

Where the family income is small—and especially in cases of long-continued unemployment—this has reduced the amount of money available for food.

The result, all too often, has been serious malnutrition.

And Dr. G. C. M. M'Gonigle, Medical Officer of Health for Stockton-on-Tees, found that, following one such transfer of population from an "unhealthy" to a healthy area, the death-rate was increased by about forty-five per cent. over a five-year period.

If similar investigations were undertaken elsewhere, it is all too likely that they would show similar results.

Isn't there a need for an imaginative approach to the problem of slum clearance—an approach that would take into account the possible effects of increasing rents—and make special provision for cases where the breadwinner of a family was unemployed?

But no; practically always slum clearance is regarded simply as a question of transferring the inhabitants of a condemned area to new homes.

It is taken for granted that they should pay more for better accommodation.

If, paying more for rent, they have not enough left for food, that is no one's affair but their own.

Probably every one of my readers could supply, from his own experience, other examples of the way in which official lack of imagination—and consequently of understanding and sympathy—has affected the everyday life of the nation.

I HEARD a man grumbling the other day. He had started a novel his wife had borrowed from the library. The story interested him. But before he could finish it his wife, not realizing he was reading it, had returned the book. And when he tried to get it out again it wasn't available.

"It's a maddening thing," he said. "I want to know what happened."

I could sympathize with him. I remember, as a boy, reading Dickens's unfinished novel, *Edwin Drood*, not knowing, when I began, that it was incomplete.

I was horribly disappointed when I came to the end of the book and discovered that it was not the end of the story.

Perhaps you have experienced the same feeling?

You may have had an hour or so to wait before an appointment and gone into the pictures— and then had to come out in the middle of a particularly exciting film.

Or you may have overheard, in bus or train, a scrap of conversation that suggested an interesting situation—and then the speakers have got out, leaving you wondering what happened next.

I am constantly hearing bits of stories.

A great many people write to me. Many of these letters contain criticism or argument, a few make suggestions; there are even a number that express agreement with something I have said.

But among the others there are usually at least one or two that tell a story, or rather part of a story, and ask for advice or help or encouragement, or perhaps for prayers.

I do the little I can for these correspondents, and there, nine times out of ten, the matter ends. There is no sequel. The story remains unfinished.

Some time ago, for instance, a father wrote to me saying that his son had left home a year or so before and had come to London.

For months he had not heard from the boy; letters sent to his lodgings had been returned marked "Gone away."

He had telephoned his son's office, to be told: "Mr. So-and-so is not here now. He has left the firm."

Naturally, the father was worried. Had his boy lost his job—and was he afraid of "sponging" on his parents? Where was he? What was he doing? Was he well?

Could I trace the boy for him and find out what were the answers to these questions?

I had received similar appeals before; I have received others since.

It is sometimes impossible to help in any way.

In this case, however, I was able to get in touch with the missing son.

Like many other young people, he was "stage

struck." He had given up a good job in order to "try his luck" in the theatre.

He was finding the life very different from what he had anticipated. But he was in a "shop" at the moment, and, though he wasn't making much money, he felt he was gaining valuable experience.

He still had hopes of seeing his name in coloured lights in the West End, though he now had a much more accurate idea of the odds against the fulfilment of his dream.

However, he had grit, or obstinacy—according to the point of view—and he meant to "stick it."

But he knew his father would disapprove of what he had done, and he did not want to tell him until he had won success enough to justify his gamble.

I think I convinced him that his silence had been cruel. He promised that he would write home.

I also wrote to the father, and told him of my meeting with his son and of what the boy was doing, and of the promise he had made me.

But I do not know whether the promise was kept. I never heard from either father or son again.

I had taken a good deal of trouble over this matter.

I should at any rate have liked to know whether or not the boy had got in touch with his parents. But no—it was another of those unfinished stories.

15

I know countless other parsons who have had similar experiences.

During the war our prayers were constantly being asked for soldiers who were seriously wounded or dangerously ill.

Often those who made these requests were unknown to us, and as, in ninety-nine cases out of a hundred, we never heard anything more, we did not know whether the men for whom we prayed died or recovered.

I am afraid that, after a time, this rather took the reality out of our prayers.

We were left with an uneasy feeling that they had been asked for in very much the same spirit as an African might ask a witch doctor to cast a spell for him.

The "magic" of prayer had been invoked. If it worked, good and well—that was finished; churches and parsons could do nothing more for them.

If it didn't work—well, they hadn't really supposed it would do much good anyway. In neither case did they think it necessary to inform us.

There are all sorts of other instances which any parson could quote.

And this thoughtlessness, discourtesy, or in-gratitude—call it by what name you will—isn't very encouraging.

We don't, of course, do our job for the sake of thanks—but it is difficult for imperfect mortals to go on trying to help when they've no idea whether or not they are being of any real service.

It is so much easier to go ahead with a good heart if you know that you are on the right road.

It is so much easier to face the difficulties and perplexities of life if you hear from people who have got over their troubles as well as from those who are still in the midst of them.

One letter saying "Thank you" or carrying a message of optimism and happiness to any one who has helped you will enable him to carry on more effectively.

"WE are all neurotics nowadays," a doctor once said to me. He was serious.

"Look at the people you meet," he went on. "See how set and anxious their faces are. Notice the little nervous tricks they've got. And think how often you hear about men and women having nervous breakdowns.

"We're all living at too high a pressure—and this is how we pay for it."

Now, I had always been accustomed to consider the neurotic as, on the whole, a pretty useless sort of person.

In my experience the people who suffered from "nerves" were, for the most part, those who had too little to do, too much time to think about imaginary troubles.

Of course, there were exceptions. I knew how strong men had broken down under the strain of war.

I knew how intense emotional disturbance sometimes had the most far-reaching psychological consequences.

But, on the whole, I thought of neurotics as self-centred, rather spineless creatures who were running away from their responsibilities.

This idea of neurosis as something almost universal was new to me.

Yet, when one thinks it over, it isn't unreasonable.

We are living at a much faster rate than our parents did. And few of us know real ease of mind. Our waking hours are haunted by anxieties.

For the most part these don't bother the young.

Youth has the power of throwing off such things, of not worrying about them. And those who have grown up in this modern world of ours have managed, in large measure, to adapt themselves to it.

But older people are afraid of many things. They are very conscious of insecurity.

They aren't sure if their jobs are safe. They see the day drawing nearer when they will be displaced by the younger generation.

Sometimes they have lost grip in their personal relations. They can't control their children any longer—they can't even understand them.

If they are in business on their own account, they are up against unceasing cut-throat competition.

There are thousands of small shopkeepers who are fighting a losing battle against the co-operative stores and the multiple shops. And they know that it is a losing battle.

There is the fear of illness—illness that will drain away what small savings have been gathered so painfully together; illness that may bring unemployment in its train; illness that would spell swift ruin to the one-man business.

There is the fear of war. When we look around the world to-day we see everywhere dark clouds of menace.

Perhaps the wonder is that there aren't more neurotics. Or are we all, as my friend the doctor suggested, neurotic without knowing it?

That is quite possible. You know the story of the old man who said to his crony: "They're all mad but thee and me, and sometimes I'm not so sure of thee." Perhaps something of the same sort is true of neurosis. We can recognize its symptoms much more easily in others than in ourselves.

What is the remedy? Or is there a remedy?

I have known people who spent hundreds of pounds going to psycho-analysts, having their subconscious turned up and aired, but not always, I am afraid, disinfected.

In much of this treatment there is far too great an emphasis upon sex.

And you can't understand the meaning of life by thinking about sex, any more than you can learn what it is like on the mountain tops by crawling through mud.

So I am not surprised that sometimes what is called "psychological help" not only isn't very helpful, but may do definite harm.

Of course, all psychology isn't like this. But even if we can find the right psychologist, only the well-to-do can afford to spend large sums on expensive treatments.

And, though there are clinics for poorer people,

these have mostly insufficient funds and long waiting lists.

Yet surely there is some way out—some way in which we can help these people, many of whom need help so very badly.

I believe that perhaps the Churches may have an opportunity here—if they will face frankly the problems that confront men and women in the modern world and try to understand their difficulties.

The Churches are certainly taking a much greater interest in such matters.

Parsons are beginning to understand that you can't preach religion in a vacuum; that Christianity must be related to the life around us, that it has something to say about our social problems—even about politics, if we give that word its true significance, and don't interpret it in a partisan sense.

Some at least of the causes that make nervous wrecks might be removed if there was more practical Christianity in the world.

Meantime, is there nothing we can do to help the individual who is bowed under a burden of fear, who suffers from an "inferiority complex," who is nervy and jumpy and irritable, and who perhaps is making a mess of his own life and bringing unhappiness to those he loves?

Often, I believe, we can help him by enabling him to understand what is wrong with him.

He will never get right so long as he believes that all the faults are in other people, or in circumstances. He must realize that, quite frequently, it is his own attitude to life that is wrong.

So I am glad that many parsons are investigating psychology. They may find much in it that they disagree with, but they will also find much that is of value, that they can use in their work.

One of the signs of the times in this connexion is the recent meeting at York, of clergymen which Professor Adler, one of our greatest living psychologists, addressed. The Archbishop of York was in the chair.

Adler's contribution to psychology is, I think, especially valuable because the keynote of his teaching is co-operation. Let us stop trying to boss other people, he says, and learn to work with them.

In marriage, for instance, neither husband nor wife should try to dominate the other.

Marriage is a partnership—a task for two. And it's no use blaming your wife—or your husband—if it's not being very successful. It is your responsibility as well.

We have the same duty of co-operation in our work and in our relation to society as a whole. We have responsibilities which we must accept with courage and good will. And we mustn't crumple up when things go wrong, or lose our temper, or start hunting for a scapegoat.

The reason that we fail in our home life, at our job, or in our relations with our fellow-men generally is very often that we are unsure of ourselves.

We have a sense of inferiority, perhaps, because, when at school, we weren't very good at games, or because of some bodily defect, or because our parents seemed to love a brother or sister more than they did us, or because we were over-shadowed by older members of the family who were stronger or more clever.

So we are shy, and diffident, and self-conscious, distrustful of our own ability; or we brag and bluster and bully to convince ourselves that we are really strong men after all.

We fly into tempers because, as children, we got what we wanted in that way; or we have illness after illness because, as children, we were petted and coddled when we were ill and sickness became a method of bidding for extra attention.

There is purpose, you see, in everything that we do—and the purpose is usually to gain some feeling of security, or of being a centre of attention; to escape from situations in which we fear we won't shine or may make fools of ourselves; or to justify ourselves, make ourselves bigger in our own eyes.

But we are pursuing that purpose in anti-social ways, and therefore we are neurotic. And we make other people neurotic. When the boss has "nerves," his subordinates get jumpy too.

If we once recognize this, however, we can fight our way out of our neurosis and gain true happiness and self-respect in co-operating with others, in accepting our responsibilities cheerfully, in helping others to accept and discharge theirs.

There is, I think, a good deal here that may aid parsons in understanding the human problems with which they have to deal. There is, indeed, a good deal that may help all of us to a better understanding of ourselves and of our own problems and difficulties.

So, in modern terms, is re-stated a piece of ancient wisdom. It isn't what happens to you that counts, it's how you meet it.

And the best way to win happiness for yourself is to try to bring happiness to others.

I HAVE been accused of "stunting" many times, particularly during my earlier days at St. Martin-in-the-Fields.

It is a charge that has always pulled me up sharply, for I hate and abominate "showmanship" in religion.

It is utterly alien to the spirit of Christ.

Our Lord was concerned with real things, with fundamental values, with the eternal verities.

The showman cares only for appearances.

He is like the politician who rouses a great meeting to a frenzy of enthusiasm by a froth of words. "Magnificent!" you exclaim. "What an orator!"

But next morning, when you recall his speech in cold blood, you realize that most of it was completely meaningless and the rest meant the wrong thing.

No parson worth his salt wants that sort of success. It should always worry him to be told that he is stunting.

But it must never make him abandon any course of action which he believes, after grave reflection, to be right.

Once he is sure of this, he must carry on. And it seems a little strange to recall to-day some of the things which were condemned as stunts a few years ago.

The broadcasting of church services, for instance, began at St. Martin's. There were many who criticized. Some of those who were most contemptuous are splendidly effective on the air to-day.

One well-known ecclesiastic, when a broadcast from his cathedral was suggested, replied that it would be impossible, because some man might listen-in with his hat on.

I was tempted to reply that many women might listen with their hats off!

That controversy is almost dead. There are few to-day who would deny the value of religious broadcasting.

We were again told that we were stunting when we decided to keep St. Martin's open all night. There was surely no stunt in that.

While there were people who wanted to come in—and there were many who did so—it seemed to us wrong to close the doors.

What if an occasional church ornament is stolen? It can always be replaced. And it is good to know that the Church may be hard at work when the parson is asleep.

But there is a world of difference between a church that all may enter if they will and a church that sets out deliberately to catch the crowd by pandering to some popular craze or apeing the methods of the house of entertainment.

It is the duty of the Christian Church to offer to all the Bread of Life. But the parson who tries to provide a circus as well has mistaken his function.

He may bring people to church by advertising a "football service," inducing the members of the local League team to sit in the front pews, and rigging up goal-posts near the pulpit.

But isn't that purely stunting? Will they come in a spirit of reverence?

They won't think of the promise: "Where two or three are gathered together in My name, there am I in the midst of them."

They will be too busy looking for Jock So-and-So, who scored a couple of goals the previous afternoon.

I am also doubtful about the new idea, now being tried out in London, of cinema services.

It may be true that there are long queues outside the cinemas every Sunday evening, while the churches are half empty. But, as has been said, a church half empty is also a church half full.

And even if there is only a handful of people in the pews, that handful has come to worship God. (I have noticed that those people whose church-going is purely formal rarely attend evening services.)

The people who throng the cinemas don't want to join in public worship. They want to see a film show.

I have no objection to that, so long as the pic-

tures they see are of a decent, healthy kind. I
would rather see young people in the cinema on a
Sunday evening than parading the streets.

But don't let us deceive ourselves by calling a
film show a cinema service.

However carefully we choose our big film,
however excellent is the moral that it points, it
remains essentially something that is intended to
entertain.

We cannot make it a sermon by adding to it a
picture of a church service, with a choir on the
sound track, and asking the audience to join in the
singing.

Films, novels, plays, all have their place, and an
honourable place, in our lives. They may all
be made to the glory of God. They may all do
His work. But their place is not in church, nor
can they serve as substitutes for public worship.

The advocates of the cinema service are making
the mistake of thinking that the important thing
is to get people to come to church—or, if they
won't do that, to attend something that may pass
for a religious service.

Our ancestors also attached importance to
churchgoing. They sought to secure it by bringing non-attenders before the magistrates and
punishing them.

We recognize the futility of that to-day. But
is it any better to try to bribe people with films,
or football teams, or any similar bait?

There is no value in church attendance unless it

springs from an honest and heartfelt desire to seek and draw near to God and obtain from that communion strength for His service.

It is no good trying to make religion easy. The Christian life can never be easy. It isn't just a case of being kind to the cat and polite to grandma.

It is a struggle against evil—the evil that is all around us and the evil that is within our own hearts.

The call to this unending conflict must have a note of sternness in it. It must be a call to self-dedication, to sacrifice.

It must make demands upon all that we have and are, not offer us a painless extraction of our sin—Christianity without the Cross.

It is related of the author of *Onward, Christian Soldiers* that his bishop objected to the line, "With the Cross of Jesus going on before," as savouring of Romish practices.

He replied by suggesting the alteration: "With the Cross of Jesus left behind the door." The bishop surrendered.

The cross is, indeed, an essential element of the Christian Life. We are all called upon to take it up.

The danger of so many of our modern schemes for "popularizing religion" is that they obscure or ignore this. They try to bring God over to our side, instead of ranging us upon His.

But we can't make a bargain with God. We can't say to Him: "We are perfectly willing to be Christians, so long as it doesn't mean anything."

We can't be Christians unless it means everything. There is no Christianity on easy terms.

If we pretend that there is, we produce a monstrous Babbitt religion. We shut out Christ and enthrone Mammon. We banish all the uncomfortable virtues, and throw over our sins the cloak of self-complacency.

"We're all good fellows together," we say—and go on selling pups to our neighbours.

I am sure that those who are now most enthusiastic about the new ideas for "presenting" Christianity would shrink in horror from such a travesty.

But that, I fear, might very easily be the practical result of their activities.

And I believe it is by placing the demands of the Christian life at their highest and most uncompromising, and not by stunts or sensationalism, that the Church will most surely appeal to those who to-day stand aloof from organized religion.

MOST of us are superstitious, though we like to pretend we aren't. If we catch ourselves boasting that our health is good or our luck is in we generally hasten to touch wood or to say "unberufen."

It is hardly for me to be censorious here, for I do both! In a sense these very absurd gestures seem called for, since Fate does seem to give us some of its nastiest blows at moments when we're feeling particularly pleased with ourselves.

Of course, actually it's no good appealing to a non-existent forest god, which is the real meaning of "touching wood," and nobody in his senses really believes that there is some other god who sits up and takes notice because we murmur a word of German.

It is, however, wise on every ground to be modest if a measure of success comes our way. We needn't get all puffed out about it. It's nothing to make a song about.

Our forefathers expressed that idea in a number of proverbs. "Pride goes before a fall." "Pride goes before, and shame follows after."

Those sayings can be traced back to a verse in the Old Testament: "Pride goeth before destruction, and an haughty spirit before a fall."

Need I give any illustrations of that? We have seen it happen in people we know, in all sorts of ways, little and big—people of whom it might be said now that they have a "great future behind them."

And there are few—if, indeed, there are any of us—who haven't uncomfortable memories that point the same moral.

We know, besides, that our fall wouldn't have been nearly so disturbing if we had been a little more modest in the hour of success.

Added to our troubles now is the unpleasing reflection that friends and neighbours are not displeased to see us taken down a peg.

History is full of cases of pride going before a fall. I wonder, by the way, how many of the dictators and would-be dictators of our modern world read history.

Most of us, as we grow older and wiser, manage to avoid the more obvious forms of pride. But that does not mean that we aren't vulnerable any more. Pride may still get us in new and subtler ways.

And sometimes now it is far more dangerous and its consequences far more destructive and disastrous. It seems reasonable and right enough that a father should be proud of his son.

We don't feel that this sort of pride is giving hostages to fortune. Well, it depends. When we make plans for our children, we may be asking for trouble.

I knew a young man who was very proud of his skill at making the worse appear the better reason, certainly he could talk the hind leg off the proverbial donkey.

He was to read for the Bar, and he dreamed of the day when his eloquence and skill in cross-examination would make him famous.

He was so sure of success that he boasted about it in advance; he shared these glamorous dreams with his friends.

His ambitions came to nothing, his father's business struck a bad patch. The money that was to have turned him into a barrister was used to keep the business afloat, he had to earn his own living straight away. It was a bad blow, but he took it like a man, he did well, but he isn't at all proud about that.

It isn't the kind of success he wanted. He told me last time I saw him that he had learned his lesson. "Pride goes before a fall," said he as he recalled his youthful ambitions.

But he hasn't learned the lesson completely. He still clings to those dreams of his—only now he has transferred them to his son.

That son is to do all the things he wanted to do himself. He is making the boy a barrister. And the youngster doesn't want to be a barrister, he isn't interested in law, nor is he suited for it.

There are thousands of fathers like that—trying to realize their own thwarted ambitions in the persons of their sons, blind to the fact that the

boys' inclinations and aptitudes lie in other direc-
tions altogether.

These fathers are preparing tragedy for themselves and their sons. That is one of the subtler
ways in which pride can get us. There are others.

You remember the Pharisee who thanked God
he was not as other men? Few of us are quite
as crude as that nowadays, but it is surprising how
many people still exist who fancy that theirs is the
only authentic way of salvation, and attempt to
impose their standards on others.

From there it is so easy for us to fall into a
form of spiritual pride, to think, for instance, that
even if we aren't exactly perfect we are anyhow
a jolly sight better than our neighbours.

Perhaps, after a stern fight, we have been able
to overcome some gross sin, while other people
whom we know and could, and alas do, name,
have not been equally successful.

So we get a kind of pride in our one achieve-
ment, and pride is invariably the prelude to a
fall.

Temptation comes in many subtle forms—it
does not always send in its card.

At the very moment we think we have done with
it, it is at our elbow congratulating us on our
victory. It wears the face of virtue. It speaks with
the voice of virtue. It has a way, too, of calling
itself Duty.

The worst sins are not always committed by
bad men. Some of them are committed by sin-

cerely religious men who think they are doing God's work.

We can have no security that we may not fall into similar error. But it may help us to avoid it if we realize its possibility, if we learn, not only to distrust our impulses, but frequently to re-examine our standards of judgment and, above all, to be humble at our condition.

That does not mean that we must never declare boldly what we believe, but only that we must perpetually remember the words of Cromwell:

"In the bowels of Christ, think it possible that you may be mistaken."

If that is our attitude, there is one sin we shall not be likely to fall into to any serious extent— the sin of pride.

No man can examine his words and his deeds, no man can check up in this way, without finding so many faults and shortcomings in himself that pride, at least, will be far from him.

"HAVE you any hobbies?" the late Sir Henry Dickens was once asked. "Seventeen grandchildren and one great-grandchild," he replied.

It was an answer worthy of the son of the great novelist, who loved children. And it may help us to realize what a hobby really is.

There are so many people who claim to have hobbies who have nothing of the sort. What they do have is a second business, pursued with the same energy and determination—and selfishness—that they expend on earning a living.

You all know men and women of the type I have in mind. They never relax; they never let up.

They play golf, or bridge, or tennis with the fierce concentration of a financier fighting for a fortune.

They hold "inquests" after every game.

They cannot even spend a day in the garden without making a task of it.

No pottering about for them. If they get out the mower after lunch they go "all out" to have the lawn finished before tea.

Roses to them mean greenfly and chemical

236

sprays. Birds are nasty little vermin that are always getting at the fruit.

Their garden is as full of annoyance and anxiety as the office—they get no rest or pleasure out of it.

And if the man next door grows a bigger cucumber, or a bigger gooseberry, or a bigger anything else for the local flower show—why, the family will be driven to think life is not worth living.

Talk to such a man and he'll justify himself by saying: "What's worth doing is worth doing well."

But what is it that's worth doing? When a doctor says—as doctors do sometimes—"You ought to take up some hobby," what does he mean?

He says it, as a rule, to the man who can't escape from his work; who takes the office home with him; who chews over, in his leisure, all the things that happened while he was on the job, and wonders whether, perhaps, he did or said the right thing.

He wants him to learn to relax.

For the man who has work to do, that is in most cases the true value and usefulness of a hobby. Its whole purpose is defeated if he takes it too seriously.

I talked to a psychologist recently.

He used a phrase that struck me—"the inner drive." I asked what he meant by it.

"There are people who drive themselves all the

time," he said, "whether they're working or playing. They can't take things easy. Usually they end by crocking up. That's one reason why there are so many nervous breakdowns."

He wasn't talking, he explained, of those who were driven by an outer compulsion—who had to work, even habitually, against time in order to finish jobs that must be done.

"You can always escape from your work," he said, "even if it's only for half an hour with a book at the end of a sixteen-hour day. But where this 'inner drive' exists it's you that's wrong. You can't escape from yourself."

So when I put the question: "Have you a hobby?" what I really ask is: "Have you something that takes you out of yourself?"

There are people, of course, who can answer quite truthfully: "Yes, my work does that." Their work is their hobby.

They are fortunate—now. But, if they are wise they will cultivate an alternative hobby against the day when they have to retire.

Otherwise, when their work is taken away from them they will be completely lost.

That applies not only to men and women in trades and professions. It applies also to the mother who is bringing up her children.

I know that's a full-time job in every sense of the term.

But—make time for a hobby. The children will go to school. They will grow up.

As the years pass, they won't make any less

demand upon your love—they'll still need that—
but they won't occupy your time as they do
now.

You'll have many empty hours on your hands—
unless you have other interests to fill them with.

These other interests, too, may help to keep you
more closely in touch with your children in the
after years.

But let me turn back to the more serious
problem—the people who, far from finding joy
in their work, make a task of everything they do.
The people who can't escape from themselves.
Who never lose themselves in anything. Who see
everything in relation to themselves.

If their "hobby," as they still call it, is garden-
ing, their garden is always "my" garden. It is
never God's garden. They do not see His handiwork in the beauty of the flowers, but only the
results of their own labour.

And that beauty is not something to be loved
for its own sake, but something to be compared
with their neighbours' display.

So, in that garden, there is always something
to do; seldom, if ever, anything to enjoy or
leisure to enjoy it.

The people I have in mind don't take any
pleasure in the actual work.

Again, a man may say: "My hobby is hiking."

You wouldn't think it possible to make a task
of walking in the country, amid all the glory of
early summer. But this man does.

He is blind and deaf to all the sights and sounds that delight the rest of us. His object is mileage.

Are you like these people? If you are, you don't have a hobby. Too many of us are like that. So we don't really have a hobby.

We haven't learned how to use our leisure properly. We haven't begun really to live.

For to most of us our daily work stands for the means of life rather than life itself (alas! that this should so often be inevitable). It is leisure that is the true test. If that is wrong, life is wrong.

I RECEIVED a letter the other day that made me cross. It was quite a harmless letter, really, but one phrase in it annoyed me.

My correspondent was talking about his parson.

"He's a real good fellow," he wrote, "but of course he's only a country parson."

"For goodness' sake," I wrote back, "never say that again. The country parson is often the best fellow in England, with the toughest of jobs."

Yet I suppose I shouldn't have been cross—the writer was only using what is, after all, a very common expression.

It is the fashion to belittle the country parson. It has been so for hundreds of years. It will probably continue to be so.

I won't say he doesn't mind; he's human like the rest of us, and he probably does.

Sneers do hurt him sometimes, but he gets on with his job, and that job is very often supremely well done. And—please note—it's one of the most difficult in the world.

Think for a moment what it means. Preaching at least twice every Sunday to half-empty pews, and sometimes to rows of people whose faces

241

look uncommonly like expressionless melons, from which no man may hope to awaken a flicker of response.

And all the time now there is the competition of broadcast services with their popular preaching and warm hymn singing, which may be heard at one's own fireside.

A country parson's Sunday is often a rather heart-broken affair: none of the electricity that, in a crowded town church, passes between preacher and congregation, none of the interest of fresh faces and new listeners.

I worked hard at St. Martin-in-the-Fields for years, but I do not think it was anything like as difficult to keep keen and faithful there as it would have been in an isolated country parish.

The work in the village is equally worth-while and a stiffer proposition. The countryman may not be easily moved by words. To him one sermon may be just like another, but he's a pretty good judge of a man, and living alongside of his parson he knows him well.

And the clergyman who wins the love and respect of the countryman is a really fine fellow. They look for deeds, not words, at Little Puddlington, and attractive preaching doesn't take the parson very far. And the Sunday services are only part of the job; not the most important part.

A parson's real work is going about the parish, loving and caring for the people—"standing by," so to speak, in the name of God.

There are hundreds of clergymen doing that work to-day. They are the salt of the Church of England. They are known to every one in the village, and everything that is to be known about them, often with ten per cent. added on, is known.

Their door is shut to none. Not a "gentleman of the road" passes the vicarage but calls on them, not one goes away without something to eat and often enough something in his pocket besides.

In the heart of some of these wanderers there may stir what is more than food and money, because the parson had time for a smoke and a talk.

Outside, in the wider world, there are young men making good in their careers because the parson saw their promise and lent a hand; and girls, once in trouble, leading happy, self-respecting lives, because the parson made sure they got another chance.

And in those moments of temptation which come to all, how many are there who remember the old clergyman—perhaps long after he sleeps in the quiet God's acre in the shadow of his church—and say "No" to the whisperings of evil. The good country parson never knows the good he does—and good never dies.

Of course, it's not all like this. There are duds in the country as well as in the town. There is a darker side, too, to the work of the country clergyman.

I do not agree with the picture of the English village in some modern novels, but you find envy, malice, and backbiting in every community. And, my word! it can flourish in a country village.

Sometimes, through no fault of his own, the parson becomes the centre of a storm.

I knew a case where a spiteful old woman, annoyed by a fancied slight, started the ball of gossip rolling, and away it went, round the village, with incredibly cruel results.

Even where the malice of gossip is spared him, the country parson has much to contend with. He is often illpaid, he inclines to a large family, needing education.

It is a constant wonder to me how he manages, as he does, to send his children to good schools and later to some university.

Also, though he loves his people, there must be moments when the country parson longs for the society of those who have the same background of intellectual tastes as himself.

That is not always to be found in the village.

As for his wife—well, I think any woman who marries a parson is a heroine, unless she has a disposition to what is called church work.

The wife of a country parson must have her special difficulties.

Finally, have you ever thought what is expected of the village clergyman?

He must have many virtues besides that of Godliness. If he is to satisfy everybody there is no grace that he can do without. He must shine at the Sunday supper in the Big House; he must know all about the crops and be able to talk about them; he must raise money to repair the church, and of course he should be a bit of a fast bowler!

To be a thoroughly good and faithful parson in the village is no easy task, and seeing that there are so many of them up and down the country I desire respectfully to sing their praises here.

Thank God for the good country parson! And so say all of us who know the life of the English countryside, and what Parson may mean to it.

The most beautiful presentation of Christianity I know is that which is offered in a little country church on a Sunday evening, where two or three are gathered together in God's name, and Parson and People are one.

I ONCE heard someone say of a gracious old lady who had just heard of the death of a friend of her school-days:—

"It must be terrible to be old like that, and to have your friends die one after another, and to think each time, 'It may be my turn next.' "

She had her back to the door and hadn't noticed the old lady come into the room. And none of the rest of us had been able to stop her. But now she turned round.

"Oh," she exclaimed. "I'm so sorry. I——"

"Not at all, my dear," said the old lady, sitting down placidly in her usual chair. "One doesn't like to lose one's friends, but when one is old one knows it is only for a little time."

I had a talk with her afterwards during her own last illness.

"I have had a very pleasant old age," she told me. "You see, I knew I was coming to the end of my journey. And I felt as I used to do when I was younger and nearing the end of a holiday.

"I wanted to make the most of the days that remained—but I was also very happy to think that soon I would be home again. Well, I'm going home now."

Whenever I hear any one talk—as people

sometimes do—of the tragedy of old age, I think of these words.

There is no terror in the shadow of death, no sadness in the thought of farewell, if we have so lived that, at the ending of our days, we can feel that we are going home.

Sometimes I think also of an old man I saw sitting in the sun by his cottage door.

He wasn't reading; there was no one near to talk to him; he was just sitting there, with his gnarled hands closed over the head of his stick.

I was very young, and I remember pitying him. How dull he must find it, I thought.

But it wasn't dull to him, as I discovered when I stopped to chat.

"It's wonderful just to be able to sit and enjoy life," he told me. "I've always been too busy before."

There are other old people I have known to whom life's evening was a time of quiet content.

I have also, of course, known some who were fretful and miserable and afraid. They were a burden to themselves and to everybody who had anything to do with them.

Yet they clung to the outworn shell of life as desperately as ever, in a shipwreck, a sailor clung to a spar.

Seeing them, I have dreaded old age—I have hoped that I should never live to be like that.

I expect that, in similar circumstances, you have felt much the same.

Nor do I have very much sympathy with the attitude that mere length of years is something admirable in itself.

There is nothing to be particularly proud of in living to be a hundred—it's how we have lived that counts, whether life ends at twenty or at seventy or outlasts the century.

Yet perhaps it is human, when all else has gone, to find what merit we can in the mere fact of survival.

You know the story of the old lady, nearing a hundred, who inquired daily for the health of a neighbour who was actually a centenarian.

One day, in fear and trembling, her family told her, as gently as they could, that this woman had died in her sleep. They dreaded the effect the news would have upon her.

But it was they who got the shock.

"Good," she said. "Now I'm the oldest woman in the street!"

But old age isn't necessarily either selfish or self-important.

Personally, I'm inclined to think that we can all make our declining years beautiful—if indeed we survive to be old—by making the best of the life we are living now.

Disraeli once wrote:

"Youth is a blunder, manhood a struggle, old age a regret."

It's a cynical summing-up of life, but too often a true one.

I might even say that it is always a true one—for those who live for themselves.

But there are still—thank God!—people who are never too busy to lend a helping hand to others, who dedicate themselves to noble causes, who are more concerned to give than to get.

I cannot think that to them old age will bring only regret.

Now, please don't misunderstand me. There are millions of people who are hard put to it to earn a bare living.

They can't do a great deal to help others—though many do do surprisingly much when a neighbour strikes a bad patch.

But even in our own homes and among our families we can be either takers or givers.

Which are you? If you answer that question honestly, you are well on the way to knowing what sort of old age you will have.

But, even if you've been a taker, rather than a giver, up to the present, there's no need to despair. There is still time to change.

I have known people who have been takers for the full period of man's allotted span—and then switched over and made the evening of life redeem its opening and prime. And so, at ninety they have found life good.

Well, some of us may live to be ninety too. And we may find life good. Or we may be forty or fifty and think it not worth living.

We live in deeds, not years; in thoughts, not
    breaths;
In feelings, not in figures on a dial.

We should count time by heart-throbs. He
    most lives
Who thinks most, feels the noblest, acts the
    best.

If the deeds and the thoughts and the feelings
are right, the years, however they stretch out,
will look after themselves.

And it will not matter whether it is early or late
that God calls us home.

WHY DODGE THE PARSON?

"THE parson's at the door," calls the woman to her husband.

"Well, tell him I'm out; tell him I'm dead; tell him I've gone to see a man about a dog; tell him anything you like, and let me know when he's gone."

In theory, the parson doesn't hear these domestic exchanges. In practice, he very often does, and though he gallantly pretends otherwise, it's a bit depressing.

The more so when he hasn't called round to collect another scalp for his denominational museum, but only to see if there is anything he can do to help generally.

Of course, this business of the local clergyman visiting what is called his flock is a delicate one.

Looked at from the clerical angle it's like this— if we do pay a friendly visit the male members of the household are liable to slip out at the back door until the coast is clear. If we don't, they are likely enough to complain that though they've lived a long time in the neighbourhood, "no parson has ever darkened the door."

From the angle of the family visited, it is, of course, quite conceivable that the minister may not be wanted.

When this is so I would respectfully suggest that the man should say so at his own front door and not shove the job on to his wife.

She's got plenty of trouble without that.

I have a good friend who doesn't like parsons. He also knows his mind and speaks it.

Recently, when the vicar called round, he told him, man to man, as they say, that he would be most happy to subscribe generously to his funds if he on his part would promise never to call again!

Well, you know where you are with a man like that.

I prefer it to the attitude of a celebrity who, on receiving a letter from me saying that if he cared for a visit I should be glad to call, replied with a fulsome letter of delight.

Months passed, years passed, and we never met.

In the end I learned from a reliable source that orders had been given that on no account was the parson to be allowed into *the* presence!

I can quite appreciate any one not wanting to see me and telling me so, but I've little use for the fellow who says how happy and blessed a thing it will be to receive a visit and then takes jolly good care that one is not allowed to cross the threshold.

I remember asking a man whether he and his sons would care to attend a men's meeting of which I was in charge.

No, he didn't think so, but he went on to say

that if there was a meeting for women he'd gladly send the missis and the girls along!

He thought—as many men do—that religion is just for women and children and invalids—not for men like himself and his sons.

"I may take it up later on," he added. Later on—when he was off the active list for good, or illness and old age had got him down.

Then a touch of religion would be quite a good thing. By no means a bad investment on the threshold of eternity.

There are thousands of men like that. For them, religion isn't a way of life, it's something it might be well to attend to just before the end. A ticket possibly for the next world, who knows?

Anyhow, they don't intend to die yet awhile. Why bother about the ticket now? Nobody can expect a man to go to the station to book next year's holiday return.

But there is one thing men forget. When they do go for their ticket they will have to take the money with them.

No money, no ticket. You can't waive the question of payment either for Hastings or Heaven. There are no free passes.

But, of course, nobody in his senses believes any longer in this ticket-for-Heaven business. Religion is not a system of rewards.

But neither is it a sort of last-minute magic that wipes life's slate clean of sins and shortcomings and presents every deathbed penitent with a certificate of spiritual health.

Christianity is a way of living, not of dying. But what an uncomfortable way of life, men say. It makes such an infernal number of demands.

If the parson comes round all friendly and human, because he desires to do what he can to help, if it's a neighbourly visit by a man of God who knows that neither he nor any man can live by bread alone, it would be more courteous, and perhaps less morally cowardly, for the man to deal with the visitor himself.

He need never see him again if he doesn't want to.

THERE was a crowd of us in the room waiting to hear the news.

We sat silent, and I think that all our thoughts had gone back to that other moment, earlier in the year, when we had waited, with sorrow in our hearts, for an announcement we knew to be inevitable. There was a curious similarity between the two scenes. There was the same sense of doom in the air, the same feeling of personal loss.

But this tragedy, which had come so swiftly and unexpectedly, seemed the more poignant. When King George died, we mourned his passing, but we felt also gratitude for the strength that had sustained him through twenty-five long years of faithful service to his peoples, and for the wisdom and selfless devotion to duty that had added new lustre to the monarchy.

What we mourned as we heard the fateful words of King Edward's message was the might-have-been. It is THAT we still mourn to-day. We had hoped so much from that simple comradeship, that warm-hearted sympathy, which brought a more intimately human touch than ever before to the ancient office of kingship.

When the reading ended there was silence in the room. No one knew what to say. But there were tears in the eyes of a young girl. One could appreciate that. There must have been many such tears. It is tragic to have to say farewell in such a way to one for whom we have so deep an affection.

We all regret King Edward's decision. I do immensely. I was one of his chaplains. I had been chaplain to his father and his grandfather. When he was young I saw him often at my father's home.

I know his charm. I know also how very real and deep-seated his feeling for human suffering has always been. I recall many a lovely and gracious thing that he has done—things that could only have been done by a man with a big heart. He remembered the "forgotten men." First as Prince of Wales, and afterwards as King, he brought home to the nation the meaning of unemployment in misery and waste of manhood and womanhood.

When most of us were talking and thinking only of returning prosperity—and prosperity was, in fact, returning over the greater part of the country —he reminded us of the depressed areas and of their call upon us.

This rich and generous humanity endeared him to millions whose lives were hard and sombre. They felt that he understood their problems. They knew that he saw things for himself, that he had moved freely among his people, that he had spoken freely with them—and they with him. They knew that he wanted, if he could, to help them—to bring hope and joy once more into their lives.

He possessed, in full measure, many of those qualities which constitutional monarchy requires, which fit kingship into the pattern of the modern democratic State and make of Sovereign and people a unity of hearts and service.

It is these things that made his abdication a tragedy.   They ensure that he will always be remembered among us with regret and affection.

He has gone from us by his own act. Even while we regret it, we must accept that act. Faced with a tragic choice, he has made his decision.

The unhappy circumstances that led him to renounce the Throne are known to us all. There is no need to recapitulate them.

But we must, I think, give due weight to one consideration. It was decisive for King Edward. The position of a constitutional monarch is of peculiar delicacy. It demands that the Sovereign shall be above the battle of parties and of factions. He must not become a centre of controversy.

King Edward had set his heart upon a project that appeared unseemly to a great multitude of his subjects, to many of them on religious grounds. There may have been an equal number who saw no harm in what he proposed to do.

The relative numbers do not matter. What does matter is that there was no way in which the King's wish could be met without making that wish a matter of public controversy both here and in the Dominions. The issue would have cut across the normal lines of party politics. It would have made of the monarchy a storm centre.

It is not the least of King Edward's services to the State that he determined this should not happen. There should, he resolved, be no party of "King's men." It meant, he knew, a choice between renouncing his project and renouncing the Throne. He made his choice. He renounced the Throne.

I do not think there is a single one among us who does not wish he might have chosen the alternative course. But the choice was not ours to make. It was his. And we must honour him for his refusal to attempt to exploit his personal popularity, the universal affection in which he was held, to gain what he desired while still remaining King.

"He behaved," as Mr. Baldwin phrased it in the House of Commons, "as a great gentleman."

His decision taken, he has tried, in every possible way, to make smooth the path of his successor, to ensure that the loyalties which centred upon himself should be transferred to his brother, who is now our Sovereign.

Yet there may be a temptation to some—especially to the younger among us—to protest that all has not yet been said; to raise the issue which King Edward himself refused to raise.

If I were a young man there might seem to be

something fine and romantic about this. And there may be those who are thinking along these lines to-day. The Constitution is so cold and lifeless a thing seen with the eyes of youth; why should one so beloved as King Edward be allowed to sacrifice himself to it?

Should such an attitude gain ground, immeasurable mischief may result. But I do not believe, I cannot believe, that it will gain ground.

Even to those who are tempted by it, there is, it seems to me, one unanswerable argument against it. King Edward would not wish it. In what he wrote to Mr. Baldwin, and again in his broadcast, he made that crystal clear. He does not wish it. The past is dead; we must look to the future.

There is also this to be said. While we deeply regret the passing of a democrat King, one who had so keen and so human an understanding of the problems of the poor and so much sympathy with them, we should remember that the King who succeeds him has given many proofs of a similar warmth of feeling.

He also knows the life of the people—has seen and felt for the sufferings of the unemployed. And he comes to the Throne, not because he wishes it, but because it is his duty.

We cannot, in the weeks and months that lie ahead, make his task light. It can never be that. But we may make his burden infinitely heavier to bear.

One word more. I think there is hardly a

mother throughout the country whose heart is not sorrowful for Queen Mary. And we all, men and women alike, feel that she must be spared further grief.

But what an example, throughout her whole life, she has set us—an example of single-hearted following the path of duty. Surely from her and from the King we may get our own cue. It is no small thing that they are called upon to do, but they do it unflinchingly.

Our duty also is clear. Let us do it as they do theirs.

I SERVE

JUST before it, a man said to me: "Why all this fuss and bother about the Coronation?"

He thought it was just a piece of "medieval tomfoolery," and as for paying to see the Coronation procession, why, he wouldn't even listen to the broadcast.

I met him again the other day. He was in high good humour. He had just secured two very good seats for the procession, he told me—and at a remarkably reasonable figure.

For a moment I was tempted to remind him of his previous remarks. However, he remembered them himself. He went on:—

"It isn't the show I want to see. But I feel we ought to be there—as many of us as can get—just to wish him God-speed. I reckon it's about the most difficult job in the world, being King of England."

This man may merely have been trying to explain his sudden change of attitude. All the same, he was right. Being King of England is one of the most difficult jobs that there are.

You know the old motto of the Princes of Wales: "I serve."

For a hundred years, ever since Queen Victoria

came to the Throne, that might have been the motto of our Sovereigns. At any rate, every one of them has lived up to it.

But it hasn't been easy. For they have all been constitutional monarchs, and that is a great deal harder than being an absolute ruler.

A king who rules as well as reigns can do what he believes to be right.

A constitutional king has to stand by while his Ministers do what he believes to be wrong.

"The Queen," wrote Bagehot, discussing the legislative veto in the days of Queen Victoria, "must sign her own death warrant if the two Houses unanimously send it up to her."

The development of representative Government, of Parliament, the party system and the Cabinet, has pared away the powers of the Sovereign.

It is the Ministers, not the King, who decide all issues.

Yet the King cannot wash his hands of it all, cannot say: "It is no business of mine; let them go on with it," and turn away to his social duties or to amusement. For he cannot divest himself of a sense of personal responsibility.

He has been called to this high office, has been set apart from other men in the loneliness of kingship.

In the eyes of millions of his subjects, especially of his subjects of other races overseas, he is thus invested with a mystical authority.

They do not appreciate the niceties of our Constitution, or its careful separation of the realities of power from its ancient symbolism.

To them the King is indeed the ruler of his people.

And even among those of our blood, living in these islands, there are many who cannot readily understand just what is the position of the Sovereign.

More than once men and women have said to me: "If only the King knew about it he would do something."

Knowing himself regarded in this way, knowing too that every Act of State is done in his name and by virtue of that royal authority he no longer wields, the Sovereign must feel responsible for much that he cannot help, which he would alter if he could.

So there has arisen what is, I believe, the most difficult, the most delicate, and the most valuable of all the functions of kingship.

The King is, in a fuller sense than any Prime Minister can ever be, the representative of all his people.

He has the right—and the duty—to speak in this capacity to his Ministers when the occasion demands it.

King George V could do this with all the authority, not only of his royal rank, but of his long experience of men and affairs, and history will testify how much his Ministers owed to him, and how, while keeping strictly within the limits of the Constitution, he was yet able to influence and to guide.

18

King George VI will be able to speak, whenever the need may arise, with more knowledge of
the problems of industry and the lives and labours
of working people than any previous Sovereign
has possessed, or many of his Ministers can claim.

In the days ahead that may prove of inestimable
advantage to the State.

More and more Governments and Parliaments
are forced to concern themselves with questions
of industrial organization. More and more it is
being realized that disputes between employers
and employed should not be decided by the harsh
arbitrament of strike or lock-out, but should be
settled in a spirit of justice, good will and common
sense.

It may be that, behind the scenes, his Majesty,
who, as Duke of York, was an ambassador of
reconciliation between class and class, will be able
to contribute something of the necessary lubrica-
tion of human sympathy.

Now please don't misunderstand me.

I am not suggesting that there has been in the
past, nor am I advocating for the future, any sort
of "interference" with the duties of Ministers on
the part of the Sovereign.

But the Constitution, as all authorities upon it
admit, while it takes away so much from our
Sovereigns, still gives them three rights of cardinal
importance.

The right to be consulted;

The right to encourage;

The right to warn.

These rights are sufficient to allow the influence of a wise and enlightened King to be a vital thing.

There is another way in which our Sovereigns have served us of which we are apt to lose sight.

The King exercises a calming and restraining influence upon party strife. The fact that his Majesty's Government, on one side of the House, is faced by his Majesty's Opposition on the other, is an insurance against such violent convulsions as have from time to time occurred elsewhere.

Both Government and Opposition have a common loyalty, and in time of emergency appeal may be made to politicians by a head of the State who is above the battle.

This can never be the case in a republic, however democratic its institutions.

Across the Atlantic, in the United States, the President may be, and at the moment is, in the very thick and centre of a party struggle.

In such circumstances, no composing or ameliorating influence is, or can be, exercised by the head of the State.

Yet America has, upon the whole, been fortunate.

We have only to look at certain other lands nearer home, from which freedom has fled and where government rests upon a foundation of terror, to realize how thankful we should be for the way in which, on our own shores, constitutional monarchy has developed.

There is one more great service, among a thousand lesser ones, which we have grown accustomed to expect from the Throne.

We look to our King and Queen for a pattern of the domestic virtues and of domestic happiness.

But we cannot appreciate this at its true worth unless we realize that this, too, presents special difficulties in the case of a constitutional King.

It has been said, and truly, that the place of such a monarch has "greater temptations than almost any other," because "all the world and all the glory of it, whatever is most attractive, whatever is most seductive, has always been offered" to him, "and always will be. "

It is hard to play the game when there are so many would-be flatterers, when pleasure beckons so enticingly, when there are so many specious "man-of-the-world" arguments to condone and extenuate every folly or "adventure."

All the more honour to those who walk unswervingly the narrow path, who are strong enough to resist temptations whose weight we cannot adequately conceive.

We cannot all attend the Coronation ceremony. We cannot all watch the procession and cheer as the King and Queen go by.

But for millions of us the miracle of wireless will make possible a more personal participation in this royal event than has ever been the case before.

And from every home throughout the King's

dominions there will go a message of good will to the Sovereign whose reign, difficult as its beginning has been, will yet, we hope, be blessed and prosperous and happy.

I HAVE just heard of the death, on the other side of the world, of a good friend who has done much to make this old earth a brighter and a cheerier place.

He wasn't a politician; he wasn't a preacher; he wasn't a scientist; he wasn't a writer. He wasn't concerned with theories.

He was just a man who loved singing—and who was able to make people want to sing with him.

Gibson Young set his world a-singing. Now, in the prime of life—not yet fifty years of age—he has passed on.

It is a good many years since I first met him, but he used to say that he and I started community singing in Britain.

He had come here from Australia, which, under his leadership, had made itself the first home of this great movement of melody.

He talked to me of the inspiration of great crowds singing as one man, of a dull, drab world that needed the saving salt of song.

To him music was as much a necessity of life as bread. He wanted to carry it everywhere.

His enthusiasm was infectious, as selfless enthusiasm always is. It got me. We started community singing in London—in the church-yard of St. Martin-in-the-Fields. It caught on right away.

Broadcasting, then in its infancy, helped it and was helped by it. What had at first seemed to some only a passing craze struck its roots down deep.

To-day, wherever a big crowd gathers, you find community singing figuring prominently on the programme.

People had sung before, of course. The old student sing-songs, which gave us "The Scottish Students' Song Book," were wonderful affairs. And many of us can remember evenings when we clustered round the piano and woke the echoes with "Clementine," "John Brown's Body"—sometimes with irreverent variations—"Polly-wolly-doodle," "Solomon Levi," and many another favourite, finishing, of course, with "Auld Lang Syne."

That students' song book, prepared originally for the Scottish universities, went all round the world.

Then there had been the war-time songs, sung by soldiers on the march or in camp.

Melodies of the moment—trifles which, in ordinary times, would have been forgotten in a year or so—were kept alive and given a haunting, poignant beauty by the power of association.

Across the years they still grip at the heart-strings.

"I shall never be able to hear 'Tipperary'

dry-eyed," a friend said to me recently. "It has been sung by too many who will never sing again."

Gibson Young found new channels in which the instinct of song could express itself—he set people singing who had never sung since their schooldays.

And he revealed to the world at large the beauty and power of melody when a multitude of voices were made as one.

Individually none of these voices might be anything to write home about; but together, in the mass, they had a quality that was unique.

And now the voice that set those millions of other voices singing is still.

One of the last times I saw him was at the Watch Night Service at St. Paul's when 1936 was ushered in. There was a great congregation inside the cathedral.

From the steps outside we tried to weld the great crowds on Ludgate Hill into a unity of song with those within. It was a hazardous experiment, but I think worth while.

I remember how we stood—Gibson and I— one on each side of the rostrum, both of us fighting asthma as we led the singing. We had to fight the crowd besides!

Like myself, he was a sufferer from asthma. But I gave him a gadget I had found exceedingly useful for it, and he was using it with great success when he went back to Australia.

For a time he was much better. Then he caught a chill and was taken to hospital. He seemed to be recovering—but one morning, when the nurse took him an early cup of tea, he was dead.

It was a peaceful ending—such as I feel, he himself would have chosen.

He is dead, but because he lived and followed his star something of sweetness and light has been brought into lives uncountable.

He journeyed through dark years—years when, at times, there seemed no hope anywhere. But he sang—and those who sang with him forgot their troubles for a while, and found renewal of strength and courage.

Such is the magic of song. In part it is due to the very act of singing, which seems to satisfy some deep-seated, primal urge within us.

In part it is because song is a link with happy childhood days, when our mother sang as she moved about the house, and we first tried our own shrill treble.

There are many of us, too, who find in song a means of getting closer to God. And how surely the Christmas carols, which we shall soon be hearing again, send our thoughts winging to the stable at Bethlehem.

If I were asked to select his epitaph, I think I should go to the poem of Sassoon's :—

Every one suddenly burst out singing . . .
. . . the singing will never be done.

These are the words that should be carved on his memorial.

But his best memorial—the one that gives the quotation its force and aptness—will be found wherever a crowd is gathered and the thousands of throats are one in the beat and pulse of a song.

WE are in danger of losing Christmas.

That may seem a strange thing to say, with shopping again in full spate and sweeping to a frantic last-minute climax.

But what I want to preserve—and what I feel is threatened—has nothing to do with shops or the splashing of money.

It is the essential Christmas—Christmas as a festival of the Church and of the family, as a season of simple homely joys and deep thanksgiving.

It is a passion of love and gratitude and good will in the heart—and no outward sign or symbol has any value unless that warm inner glow shines through it.

I once heard a story of two taximen who had a minor accident round about Christmas.

"Where the devil do you think you're going?" demanded one of them. Only he didn't say it quite so politely as that.

The other, noticing a seasonable decoration on his car, replied reproachfully: "Wot's the good of 'olly on your bonnet if you don't 'ave 'olly in your 'eart?"

What indeed? And what's the good of any of

the other "trimmings" of Christmas if we lack the spirit that gives them life?

I'm afraid sometimes that all our elaborate keeping of Christmas—our exchange of gifts, our electrically illuminated trees, our turkey and plum pudding and mince-pies—has ceased to have any real meaning.

We have forgotten the cradle in the manger at Bethlehem and the Christ Child at His mother's breast. Or we remember them only as picturesque decorations, material for pretty pictures in illustrated magazines, or an excuse for village children to sing carols out of tune.

How many of you go to church on Christmas Day? How many of you read the story of the coming of Christ to your children? How many of you even think of the tidings of great joy that came to the shepherds as they watched their flocks or brought the kings of the East to worship a new-born Babe in a humble stable?

Perhaps as a parson I'm prejudiced, but it seems to me that a secular Christmas is the worst sort of paradox.

I like, too, to think of Christmas as the family festival. I don't care much for the idea—which seems to be increasingly attractive to numbers of people—of eating Christmas dinner in a restaurant or spending the holiday at an hotel.

But it's better—anything would be better—than gathering together for a series of good old family rows.

I've known families where that happened—
where brothers and sisters had drifted apart, and
the in-laws just couldn't get on with anybody
—and still they went on meeting at Christmas
time.

They called it keeping the family together. But
where people have nothing in common but
mutual dislike they're much better to keep apart.

If you can't bring love and understanding to the
family Christmas—keep out!

That doesn't mean you should allow a quarrel
to keep you away from the old folk's fireside. Go
home by all means if you want to make it up.
Don't let pride or pique stand in the way. And
don't be afraid you won't be welcome.

If you're really in earnest about making friends,
a hundred to one you'll be met halfway. Perhaps
more than halfway.

When the Prodigal Son came home, his father
ran out to meet him.

But don't go home just to continue the fight
where you left off—to carry the quarrel a stage
further.

The family Christmas, in these circumstances,
is nothing but a mockery.

And Christmas presents are a mockery unless
there is love in the gift.

A young man once showed me, in a moment of
confidence, what he called his "Christmas
drawer." It was packed full of unwanted gifts.
Each, he pointed out, had its own neat little label

attached, showing from whom it had been received.

"You see," he explained, "I send them all out again. Then I don't need to buy presents. And the labels keep me from sending anything back to the person I got it from."

Alas, one year a mischievous younger brother changed the labels, and the tie he had presented the previous Christmas was returned to Cousin Jack, while Uncle Joe got back his fountain pen.

I'm afraid I wasn't very sympathetic when I was told of this "tragedy." I hated the cold-bloodedness of such a method of dealing with Christmas presents. Giving that isn't warm-hearted is valueless.

And the more good will we put into our gifts, the fewer unwanted presents there will be. When we send someone a Christmas token out of real affection, we think when we buy it. We ask ourselves: "What would he like?"

That's the only satisfactory way of doing Christmas shopping—to go out, if we are lucky enough to have finance, to get gifts for the people to whom we want to give, and to buy each individually, with some particular person in mind.

And if some of the gifts we receive are un-suitable—things we don't want or can't use—don't let's send them to anybody who will probably hate them just as much as we do. Provided that they will be of real use to someone let them go where they will help or give pleasure.

We can send them, for instance, to the Personal

Service League, or to some church in the depressed areas or in a poor district. And if we can afford it, let us send a cheque or a postal order along with them.

Christmas very often means most to those who have least to rejoice about. And there are thousands of homes to which very little would bring a gleam of happiness.

I could almost wish, indeed, that this Christmas we might wash out all presents among friends and relatives by mutual consent—except, of course, presents to children—and send the money we would have spent on them to make a real Christmas for those whom life has dealt with hardly.

That would, however, create loss and unemployment elsewhere.

But don't, for God's sake, let us just give to those from whom we expect to receive. Don't let us have a calculating Christmas. And don't let us spend so much time and energy fussing about "trimmings" that we lose sight of the reality of the great Birthday.

I know that, on Christmas Day, the old magic will be upon us and there will be peace and joy and good will in our hearts.

But then it will be too late to take back those harsh and wounding words we said to an overtired shop assistant, or to do anything for those less fortunate than ourselves beyond being vaguely sentimental about them.

That's why I'm writing like this now—to plead

for the Christmas spirit, not only on the day, but in our preparations for it.

There's still time for those of us who are well off to "adopt" a poor family, either on our own doorstep or in the depressed areas. There's still time to bring gladness to those for whom, unless we remember them, the message of the Christmas bells will be only a bitter mocking.

Above all, remember that Christmas is the festival of the Child. If a single little one in Durham or South Wales is shut out from Christmas joys there will be a shadow over all our merrymaking.

THE NEW YEAR AND YOU

THE Old Year has only a few more days to go; the New Year is already knocking at the gate.

As we sit by the fire, waiting for the midnight chimes, or join with our fellows in a Watch Night service in the House of God, we will think of events that have rocked the world. But we will think most of all, perhaps, of the happenings that are personal to ourselves.

Great events, though they fill the pages of history, are but the background of our lives. Every man is the centre of his own stage.

He may be tossed this way and that by forces he does not understand and can in no wise control, but he still wants to know what there is for dinner, and grumbles if it isn't done the way he likes it.

And when he falls in love, or a child is born to him, the whole universe stands still.

It is good that we should celebrate New Year's Day. It is good for us to be brought up, periodically, against the fact that time is a river, carrying us on relentlessly.

It is so easy to forget that—to live in the present, as if it were everlasting.

But here we have at least the illusion of a definite break. A year has gone, or almost gone. The last sands are running from the hour-glass.

Another year is about to begin. What have we done with the twelve months that are behind us; what shall we do with the twelve months that lie ahead?

We ask ourselves these questions, as other men and women are doing all over the world; as men and women have done for long centuries.

But how do we answer them? Do we tot up, as shrewd, selfish, good-natured Samuel Pepys used to do, sitting over his Diary on December 31, what money we have made and what we have spent, and how much we have put away for a rainy day?

Do we think of what worldly ground we have gained—or of what we hope to gain in the New Year?

Some of us, doubtless, do, and find cause for self-congratulation.

Or do we answer in the spirit of Christina Rossetti when she wrote:—

New Year met me somewhat sad:
　　Old Year leaves me tired,
Stripped of favourite things I had,
　　Baulked of much desired:
Yet farther on my road to-day,
God willing, farther on my way.
New Year coming on apace,
　　What have you to give me?

Bring you scathe or bring you grace,
Face me with an honest face,
    You shall not deceive me:
Be it good or ill, be it what you will.
It needs shall help me on my road,
My rugged way to heaven, please God.

Are we, like her, travelling the rugged way to heaven? Are we nearer to God than we were a year ago?

I'm not worrying about churchgoing or the formal profession of any creed or religion. We may go to church every Sunday for half a century and be no nearer God at the end than at the beginning.

In saying that I'm not depreciating public worship. But no form of religion can give us more than we bring to it. It is in our hearts, not on our knees, that we draw nearer to God.

Well, what is the answer?

Perhaps, for some of us, it is that we are farther away than we were from God and the things of God. We have been so caught up in worldly affairs, in the mechanics of business and daily life, that we have had no time even to think about God.

Yet God is the one Reality—the things we seek and strive for so incessantly that we shut Him out are only fleeting shadows.

I'm not saying that we can shut our ears to the demands of life, or that we have to turn our backs on the things of every day in order to find God.

Indeed, we cannot serve God in a vacuum. We must serve Him among our fellow-men, and part of our service to Him is through service to them.

As the New Year chimes fall upon our waiting ears, let us dedicate ourselves to that double duty —to our brothers on earth and to our Father in Heaven. And let us pray for strength and guidance that we may perform it.